A HISTORY OF
WESTERN SCULPTURE
CONSULTANT EDITOR
JOHN POPE-HENNESSY

Classical Sculpture

Other volumes in the series

Medieval Sculpture

Author Roberto Salvini

Sculpture
Renaissance to Rococo

Author Herbert Keutner

Sculpture
19th & 20th Centuries

Author Fred Licht

A HISTORY OF
WESTERN SCULPTURE

CONSULTANT EDITOR

JOHN POPE-HENNESSY

Classical
Sculpture

George M.A. Hanfmann

NEW YORK GRAPHIC SOCIETY
GREENWICH, CONNECTICUT

153965

© GEORGE RAINBIRD LTD, 1967

This book was designed and produced
by George Rainbird Ltd
2 Hyde Park Place, London, W.2

House editor: Jocelyn Selson
Designers: Ronald Clark, Bruce Robertson and
    George Sharp
Picture research: Linda Knelman and Enid Gordon
Map: John Flower
Indexer: H. V. Molesworth Roberts

Printed by Jarrold & Sons Ltd, Norwich, England

Library of Congress Catalogue Card Number 67–11105

Printed in Great Britain

IN MEMORY OF PAUL J. SACHS

Paul J. Sachs passed away on 17 February 1965. His love of art was as contagious as his generosity to young scholars was unbounded. The dedication of this volume inadequately acknowledges a great debt.

'*The far-famed Limper* [*Hephaistos*] *kneaded of earth the likeness of a shy maiden . . . Athena put on her head a crown of gold . . . with creatures of land and sea . . . so life-like that they seem to live and talk.*'

HESIOD

'*Many wonders there are but none more wondrous than man.*'

SOPHOCLES

'*Now we see in the image what is good and we hold the good of the image . . . but now we do not see Him; we shall see Him when the image has passed away and the Truth will come.*'

ST AMBROSE

ILLUSTRATION CREDITS

The publishers are greatly indebted to Professor Hanfmann for the loan of many photographs which would otherwise have been unobtainable. Listed below are additional sources, copyright-owners (in italics) and photographers. Miniature pictures marked ★ are alternative views of the main picture obtained from a different source. Small Roman numerals indicate introduction pictures, large Roman numerals colour plates. All other illustrations have arabic numerals.

LONDON *British Museum* 32, 70, 124, 130, 134, 136, 153, 163, 162, 173★, 187, 213, 269, 324; *Otto Fein* (photo) 325; *Guildhall Museum* 301; *F. L. Kenett* (photo) 104, 123, 126, 127; *A. F. Kersting* (photo) 135; *Professor James Mellaart*, Institute of Archaeology, 1; *Novosti Press Agency* 218; *George Rainbird*, Picture Point (photo) II, Derek Witty (photo) 122, 125, 132, 173; *Thames and Hudson* VIII (photo Georgina Masson)

MADRID *Museo del Prado* 216

MALMö *Allhem, A. B., Publishing House* (photo Jan Mark) 195, 197, 202, 212, 215

MARBURG *Bildarchiv Foto Marburg* 35, 38, 73★, 96★, 98, 111, 154, 164, 168, 169

MUNICH *Direktion der Staatlichen Antikensammlungen* 53, 107, 170, 196, 244; *Hirmer Verlag* I, III, 5, 8, 11, 12, 51, 52, 59, 87, 92, 95, 105, 112, 144, 145, 146, 161, 174, 185, 220, 234, 246, 261, 314, 334★, 336, 337, 338, 339, 340, 341, 344, 346, 347, 348

NAPLES *Soprintendenza alle antichità delle province di Napoli e Caserta* 285, 286

NEW DELHI *Archaeological survey of India* 329

NEW YORK *Walter C. Baker Collection* 7, 46, 229; *Tet Arnold von Borsig* (photo) 204; *Metropolitan Museum of Art* iv, 17, 20, 22, 27, 219, 227★, 253; *Norbert Schimmel Collection* V; *Paul Woolf* (photo) 44

NICOSIA *Cyprus Museum* 13

PARIS *Archives Photographiques* 249; *Bibliothèque Nationale* 120, 121, 272; *Photographie Giraudon* viii, 90, 91, 224, 235, 256★, *Jean Roubier* (photo) 331; *Roger-Viollet* (photo) 256

PRINCETON, N. J. *Princeton University* 320

RABAT *Musée des antiquités Pré-Islamiques* 264, 289

ROME *Anderson* [*Mansell* London] 175★, 199, 230, 258, 282, 294, 295, 296, 307, 308, 318, 334; *British School at Rome* 310; *Deutsches Archaeologisches Institut* 110, 148, 210, 225, 241, 263, 282★, 284, 299★, 335, 345; *J. Felbermeyer* (photo) vii, 189, 190, 191, 192, 193, 198, 226, 238, 239, 240, *Fototeca di Architettura e Topografia dell'Italia antica* 147, 292; *Gabinetto Nazionale fotografico* 152, 311, 317; *Fondazione Ing. C. M. Lerici* 205; *Oscar Savio* (photo) [*George Rainbird* London] IV; *Soprintendenza alle antichita di Roma* 114, 115

ST GERMAIN-EN-LAYE *Musée des antiquités nationales* 273

STOCKHOLM *Professor Patrik Reuterswärd* VII

STUTTGART *Württembergisches Landesmuseum* 181

SYRACUSE *Soprintendenza alle antichità della Sicilia* 55, 81

TEHERAN M. Anvar (photo) [*George Rainbird*, London] 274, 277

TOKYO *Sakamoto Photo Research Laboratory* 278 (by courtesy of the *Cleveland Museum of Art*), 330

TRIESTE *Civici Musei* 333

VATICAN CITY *Vatican Museum* 159, 175, 227, 242, 287, 288, 306, 312

VERSAILLES *Service de documentation photographique* ii, 77, 103, 251

VIENNA *Kunsthistorisches Museum* 133, 243, 271; *Österreichisches Archaeologisches Institut* 304, 316

WASHINGTON, D.C. *Dumbarton Oaks Collection* 117, 250, 332

WORCESTER, MASS. *Art Museum* 106, 206, 207

YORK *Yorkshire Museum* 323

ZÜRICH *Walter Dräyer* 203

ACKNOWLEDGEMENTS

Those who believe in sculpture will not question the need for a series which presents in a broad view the development of this art in the Western world. I am grateful to the editor, Mr John Pope-Hennessy for his keen interest in the improvement of this volume. Miss Jocelyn Selson and her staff have wrestled valiantly with the complexities of transatlantic co-operation. Mrs Wellington F. Scott did much to make this book possible, and I was also helped by Miss Karen Zamecnik, Miss Sally Loomis, Mrs Peter Doeringer, and Mrs Ilse Hanfmann. To the many colleagues who have patiently responded to my requests and inquiries I owe profound thanks.

G. M. A. H.

CONTENTS

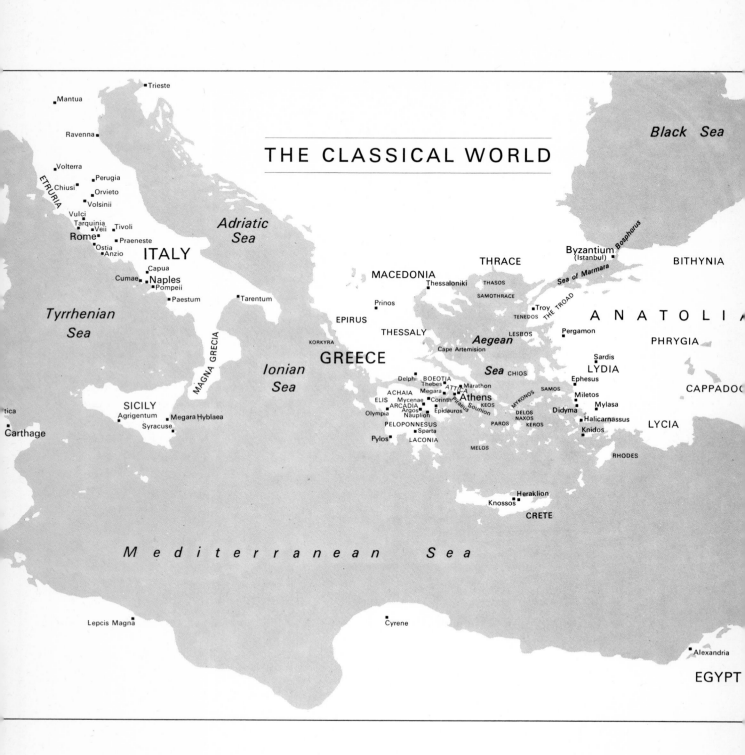

THE CLASSICAL WORLD

INTRODUCTION

'Let there be sculpture.' Epstein's brave cry disclosed to a heedless world the agony of a homeless art. Modern apologists for sculpture look back with romantic longing to the Greeks and Romans. But sculpture became the leading art of Classical civilization not by volition, not by a conscious 'heroic gesture' – the concept would have struck the ancients as hybristic – but through a unique configuration of technological, spiritual, intellectual and aesthetic forces in Egypt, the Near East and the Mediterranean. The historical situation which led the Greeks to sum up their culture in their sculpture can no more be recaptured than that Golden Age of mankind which Classical antiquity from Hesiod on so wistfully conjured.

Nevertheless, even now, when the Classicistic notion of 'ideal beauty' has been dethroned, and the objective of 'lifelikeness' at which Greek sculptors aimed has been taken over by photography, the embodiment of Greek belief in man remains a challenge to all sculptors. Those who attack 'the Classical prejudice' are as much haunted by it as those who call upon sculptors to emulate its 'vitality'. The purpose of this essay is not to proclaim any excellence of standard but to indicate something of the process by which Classical sculpture arose and declined. Later volumes of this series will show the pervasive, ever-changing impact the Classical tradition had upon Western sculpture and indeed upon Western concepts of God and man.

The forerunners

Recent discoveries have made it possible to view the arts of the Late Stone Age from Iran to the Balkans as a coherent chapter in the history of art. From that time, the development of sculpture in the Eastern Mediterranean was continuous. The most remarkable manifestations of Neolithic sculpture, painting and architecture are found in the Near East, but the same culture extended over Greece, where villages appeared in the seventh millennium and planned towns developed in the sixth millennium at such places as Knossos and Corinth which were to become famous in the later history of Greece.

The evolution in Greece from hunting, fishing and the gathering of food plants to a settled agricultural life took at least three thousand years. Sculpture is found scattered through the dwellings, some of which may have served as shrines. Figurines of domestic animals are not uncommon, but the keen concern with wild animals which had engaged the spiritual and artistic resources of the Old Stone Age no longer obtains. What survives as a central theme is the adoration of the Woman Who Gives Birth, who miraculously perpetuates the life of the race, and by analogy gives life to animals and plants. She is usually shown as pregnant.

Clay is the favoured material, but first soft, then hard stones are carved with skill. The figurines vary from an inch to as much as ten. They are not made to stand; their round volumes and smooth surfaces appeal to the hand; they are 'amulets' to be handled in ritual. Red or yellow polished colours add supernatural radiance to the heavy, 'essential' forms. The very summary, often bird-like, heads waver between hypnotic somnolence and piercing wildness. The undifferentiated physical appeal meets the creed of those modern sculptors for whom the 'essential sculpture' of geometric masses is a symbol of 'universal and everlasting meanings'.

Against this ponderous assertion of regeneration of the flesh, some extraordinary works formulate themes which are to become the glory of Greek sculpture. The village of Hacilar in south-western Turkey boasted in the fifth millennium a school of sculpture whose achievements rise far above the level of prehistoric idols. The slender grace of Lehmbruck or Michelangelo's eloquence of earthbound body awakening to life come to mind when one views the group of woman and youth (1): she compassionate in surrender, he vibrant with youthful, almost Parthenonian energy. Equally amazing is the *Neolithic statuette from Lerna* (i). Both sculptors break away from the dominant concern with fertility to celebrate the beauty of the entire body. Despite soft, boneless forms, they strive to achieve noble proportions, and presage that sense of tectonic order which Classical Greece was to stress.

Toward the end of the Late Stone Age and in the Early Bronze Age (third millennium before Christ), the relative uniformity of cultural and aesthetic expression disperses into regional multiplicity. In some ways, the seated man from Thessaly (2) is of the Late Stone Age, but the gesture suggests an awakening of mood and thought in this distant ancestor of Rodin's *Thinker*.

Sea, sun, rock and wind – this is the world of the Cycladic Islands whose inhabitants pioneered long voyages over the purple sea. Here is the home of Greece's finest marble, the Parian, and of emery which made it possible to cut hard stone with soft copper tools. This explains the use of marble, but no environmental explanation suffices to explain why out of the voluminously fleshed Woman of the Late Stone Age the Cycladic sculptors developed

i *Neolithic statuette from Lerna* 4th millennium B.C. terracotta 0·182 m. Corinth, Archaeological Museum

Cycladic head c. 2000 B.C.
marble 0·355 m.
Paris, Louvre

images of uncompromising, crystalline abstraction (3). Such icons sometimes reach almost life-size, and were perhaps made to lie in the grave and protect the dead (ii). Did something of the geometric bias of these marble sculptors come to life a thousand years later when Cycladic sculptors created the first monumental statues for historic Greece?

Crete of the high peaks is a world of its own, a mountainous hub of sea lanes between Africa, Asia and Europe. By the second millennium its seafaring Minoan culture reaches the level of city states long established in the Near East. The religious and secular functions, the riches of the land are concentrated in palaces whose artisans transform imported materials into luxury goods for the enhancement of courtly life. Minoan art is uneven; it seeks to adopt to its own ends the ready treasury of sophisticated forms developed over a thousand years in Egypt and Mesopotamia; yet it has its own genius. Life as flow and motion is the insight Cretan artists seek to express. The youth tensed in adoration (7), the praying woman (6), a vision of swaying volumes so unlike the perennial stability of her Near Eastern prototypes; and the bull-jumping youth (5) flung into space with a boldness unrivalled until the Baroque – have a freedom, a quality of momentary fleetingness of time unique in ancient art.

An international mode of elaborate narration had developed in the Near East in painting and relief. Its essential components were derived from the Egyptian canon but with some Mesopotamian features in the rendering of landscape. To this style the Minoans bring their sense of dynamic motion and a pantheistic vitality of animals and plants. The reliefs of sacred precious vessels carved in soft stone are unparalleled in Egypt or Mesopotamia, each revealing the adventurous spirit of Minoan sculptors – sacral athletic games, the towering rise of a mountain sanctuary (8–9), and elsewhere a Brueghelian procession of harvesters. The relief is low, but the continuous dispersion of curving, moving forms and deep graven strokes creates an effect of visual oscillation not found in any other art of the second millennium B.C.

Sometime in the late third millennium B.C., Greek-speaking peoples began to enter the Greek mainland. From *c.* 1600 B.C. fortified palaces rise at places famous in Greek legends: Mycenae, Tiryns, Pylos, Thebes, Iolkos. For three centuries, these 'Mycenaeans' rule the seas and trade with Egypt and the Levant. Then their palaces go up in flames, and during the 'Dark Ages' (*c.* 1250–1000 B.C.) this Protohistoric Greece fades, its memory preserved only by myth and epic poetry.

Even more strikingly than Minoan Crete, Mycenaean art and culture display the phenomenon of 'premature exposure'. Thus such an important achievement as literacy (the so-called 'Linear B') was acquired, then lost. As with writing, so in arts: the attempt to emulate the sophisticated artistic expression of Minoan palace culture was confined to a small group, and there is a gap between the luxury arts (goldsmiths' work, ivories) of the courts and the 'popular' level (terracotta figurines).

There may be detected in Mycenaean art a tendency towards geometric, tectonic arrangement and a desire for monumentality anticipating artistic attitudes that came to fruition in historic Greece. The integration of architecture and sculpture in the famous Lion Gate relief at Mycenae (10) has monumental grandeur. The sturdy uprightness of the boy from the region of Sparta (11) is closer in spirit to Archaic *kouroi* (50–3) than to Minoan youths (7). Portraits of rulers (12) and divine images (15) have an angular energy absent from the floating, sketchy Minoan faces. So far unique are the two-thirds life-size clay statues from the sanctuary of Keos (14) and the haunting head from Mycenae (I). These are sporadic manifestations of an attitude different from the Minoan; but in general, Mycenaean art is an uneven provincial version of the Minoan.

Geometric sculpture of Greece

During the three centuries (*c.* 1000–700 B.C.) between the age of the migrations and the beginning of strong contacts with the Near East, profound social and economic changes took place. The kingships declined; landed aristocracy took the lead. Its ideals of martial heroism are mirrored in the *Iliad*. Towards the end of the period, trade and colonization emerge as leading concerns; something of this change is caught in the *Odyssey* which also gives us the first description of that political unit definitive for Greece – though still monarchic, the city of the Phaeacians is a seafaring city state.

Throughout this period the major gods and goddesses gain in importance and their sanctuaries become the focal points of Hellenic life. Athena replaces the kings on the Acropolis; Apollo at Delphi establishes moral norms and leads the Greeks overseas; while Zeus of Olympia achieves Panhellenic validity with the Olympic Games ('founded' in 776 B.C.). At the same time, Greek culture is stamped forever by Homer's creation of an Olympus of gods beautiful and immortal but intensely human.

The great creation of art in this 'Age of Epic' is the Geometric style. If by 'Geometric' we understand precise arrangement of non-organic forms in two dimensions, then no style has better earned the name; it was less concerned with order in three dimensions. Its finest expression is surface decoration of vases; sculpture was a subordinate art. Virtually all Geometric figurines known are small in scale, things to be handled or stood on shelves or benches or even hung on trees. Many were made as decorative attachments for cauldrons, tripods and other utensils (30). They claim no independent environment or 'space'. The great majority of these terracottas and bronzes were given as presents to the gods; the only truly monumental creations, the cauldrons and tripods, were cherished possessions of nobles' houses and prizes for games.

The earliest and most continuous themes are animals: stags (16, 18), bulls and horses (17). Only in animal figurines does there seem to have been a tradition from Mycenaean times, and it is animals which show the most successful translation of the Geometric sense of order in three dimensions. They are shorthand signs of existing things, but the best artists manage to inject striking observations: the deer and nuzzling fawn (18) are touching and convincing.

ii *Treasury of the Athenians, Delphi*
500 B.C. marble

15

Side by side with discipline there is often manifest a wild and chaotic energy, something like the Homeric *thymos*, signifying life-power, but also the emotion which compels men to act. This uncontrolled vitality is often seen in terracottas, but even in bronzes it seems to be the reason why human beings are often much less successfully geometricized than animals. It is curious that the major types of human figurines – the nude women, the spear-swinging warrior, the charioteer (19–21) derive from Near Eastern geometric styles. Towards the end of the period there is much experimentation with bolder motifs, with complex motion, even with Manneristic elongation (22–3, 30). But as the Geometric system recognized the figure only as a symbolic sign, not as direct 're-presentation', there was no way out except by a breakthrough to a totally different concept of reality. Homer had set before the Greeks gods and heroes larger and more glorious than life. Now the Greek sculptors led the way in the task of equalling and rivalling this Homeric reality.

Archaic sculpture

'To any vision must be brought an eye adapted to what is seen' (Plotinus). Once the assignment to create lifelikeness was turned over to photography, European artists and art critics recognized the beauty of Archaic abstractions. An entire generation of European sculptors sought to appropriate its values (Bourdelle, Mestrović, Gill); and its form and spirit became a standard designating not only a formal stage but an attitude toward reality which was recognized in other 'archaic' arts – in Early Chinese and Early Romanesque, in Early Mesopotamian and Early Egyptian sculpture.

If we view its beginning and its end, the achievement of Archaic sculpture is clear. It had started *c.* 700 B.C. from small figurines and decorative appendages. By the time the war with Persia broke out (494 B.C.), all major sanctuaries, civic centres and cemeteries in Greece had been populated with statues in the round ranging from half life-size to colossal scale. The major types had been firmly defined – pre-eminent among them the standing nude youth or *kouros* (26, 29–34, 50–2, 53, 55) and second to him the *kore*, standing maiden, fully clothed (25, 36–8, 61–2, 64–9). Although less popular with the Greeks, the seated statue, symbol of authority, had developed a continuous tradition (70–2, 74).

Action figures such as the fighting warrior or wrestling hero (20, 54) and the horseman (59) were more in vogue in minor arts and architectural sculpture (56–8, 78, 79, 86–92; II). Among the many Near Eastern animals and monsters which had excited the imagination in Archaic times, the lion (39–44) and the sphinx (47–9) acquired special importance as guardians of sanctuaries and funerary monuments.

The challenging problem of placing sculpture in architectural context was worked out in step with the development of the canonical types of the Greek temple. By the end of the Archaic period, the Doric and Ionic orders had emerged with what we still regard as normative solutions. Both filled triangular pediments with sculptures in the round (79), but the Ionic temple incorporated a long uninterrupted band of relief frieze in its superstructure (86–9), where the Doric shrine displayed the more tectonic but confining sequence of rectangular frames (metopes) permitting only two- or three-figure scenes (iii, II, 92). Statues placed at the corners of the roof and on top of the ridge-beam (acroteria), added vertical accents against the sky (80). Other solutions had been tried (79, 84–6). The canonical combination represents a victory for the architectural element; it respects the unity of major architectural parts, of platform, wall and roof. Conversely, sculptural feeling for rounded volumes was triumphant in places where transition from one major part of the structure to another is made, in the justly celebrated Greek architectural profiles. This feeling is also expressed in the rounded forms of the capitals (and, in the Ionic order, of the bases) of columns. That the column or even the entire temple is a likeness of the human figure is an Archaic theory stemming from the religious symbolism of Egyptian architecture; the Greeks transformed it into an aesthetic concept on the Pythagorean assumption that divine geometry is manifest in both.

A similar but more limited problem was worked out in funerary monuments. Here the most ambitious solution gave priority to sculpture with an incompletely framed relief decorating the main part, and sculpture in the round crowning the tall, slender pillar (iv).

The great medium of the Early Archaic phase (650–600 B.C.) was painted terracotta; it continued eminent in Corinth and in the Greek colonies in Italy (45, 47, 60, 81). Bronze served primarily for figurines and decorative attachments. By the end of the sixth century B.C., the Greeks had sufficiently mastered bronze-casting techniques to cast life-size statues, but had not yet fully realized the plastic potential of the medium. The most impressive piece of Greek *toreutike* is not the life-size *kouros* recently found in the Piraeus, but the gigantic cauldron of Vix (90–1).

The leading material of Archaic sculpture is marble, and never was it more lovingly treated. The earliest Greek marble sculptors had learned all the essentials of monumental stone sculpture from Egypt: how to start from a rectangular block with carefully dimensioned and proportioned drawing on each side; how to take the stone off 'coat by coat' with patient chisel work, thus keeping complete control and evolving the statue gradually; how to bestow the final gleam by abrasives – but marble is the one stone the Egyptians did not work, and it takes much experience to master it. What inspires awe and awakens joy is not the virtuoso technique, although it was attained

I Archaic Greece
Dioscuri, Linus, Orpheus and the Argo c. 560 B.C.
Delphi, Museum

in Late Archaic art; it is the evocation of life which yet leaves the beauty of the material intact. Swelling, modulated volumes are overlaid by lyric linear patterns (34, 48, 64), or set off against firm plastic arrays of hair and garment (35, 49, 52, 59, 67, 69), but marble never becomes flesh. Strong colours enhanced the generalized vitality of the eyes and emphasized the decorative character of locks and garments (68, III).

Archaic sculpture exhibits a determined progression towards a rendering of the human body which appears to become ever more natural. This aspect hypnotized students of Archaic sculpture well into the twentieth century. It was important; the Greeks thought it important; but it was not the whole story. Competence in anatomy does not make a work of art. As in philosophy and science, so in sculpture the Greeks integrated a relatively small amount of observation into a preconceived, deductive system. The basic intuition of the Geometric period, that the world is a geometric order, remained valid; only now geometric volumes and rectilinear motion were used to create three-dimensional sculpture.

The Archaic world

In political, social and economic history, the seventh and sixth centuries B.C. were a period of excitement and expansion, of seafaring and colonization and revolutionary change. The rule of the agrarian aristocracy declined. At the end of the period Athens was well on its way towards becoming the most democratic democracy ever known. In the sense of widening horizons, of wondrous far-away lands, Archaic Greece and the Early Renaissance are akin; but the Renaissance believed that it revived and rediscovered. In Archaic Greece things were thought of or done for the first time – philosophy, natural science, geography, medicine, history – all the effects of the 'Birth of the Mind'. Despite these advances of rationalism, the Archaic Age was religious, often desperately so: the doctrine that gods are envious of human eminence was a major tenet of Archaic life. Against Apollonian moderation and the advance of moral standards there were outbreaks of 'the Irrational', best known from the Dionysiac movement. Gods were near and could appear in human form. We may doubt whether the Parisians of the République really accepted as a divinity a young opera-singer seated on the high altar of Nôtre-Dame to represent the goddess of Reason (Fred Licht, *Sculpture: 19th and 20th centuries*). In Archaic Athens the tyrant Peisistratos was brought back from exile by a tall and beautiful Thracian flower-girl who impersonated Athena – successfully, for the Athenians 'full of astonishment received Peisistratos back' (Herodotus, 1, 60; Aristotle, *Athen. Polit.*, 1, 14).

Rich aristocratic families (iv) and wealthy merchants led the patronage; it

is less clear for how much the State accounted. Probably most of the temples and cult images were its responsibility. The *Argive Twins* are an early State dedication (34). The sphere of State-sponsored sculpture was widened when, during the sixth century B.C., it became customary to celebrate athletic victors with statues donated by the State.

Function of sculpture

In this Archaic world whose outlook ranged from Pythagoras' harmony of the spheres to outbreaks of maenadism, from the untrammelled despotism of the tyrants to the communal living of the Spartans, sculpture became the leading expression of the most essential concerns. Its functions were clearly defined: to fashion the images of gods, to adorn their temples and sanctuaries, to create presents for them, to represent the divine world and the heroic past in myths and legends, and to commemorate the dead. All of these functions of sculpture had existed in Egypt and to a lesser degree in Mesopotamia. The difference lay in the Greek belief that beauty is pleasing to the divine and that the human body is the most beautiful thing known. It is the common bond of gods and men; but divine bodies do not grow old or die. Youth and beauty are thus divine. '*La Grèce n'a inventé ni la joie ni la jeunesse, mais elle en a inventé la gloire*' (Malraux). The same *kouros* may be Apollo, or an offering to Apollo, or the memorial of a dead man. Scholars disagree whether the dedication by Aeakes is Aeakes or the goddess Hera (71).

That Archaic statues were thought to be endowed with magic life is alleged by many modern and some ancient writers, but this fairy-tale motif is not unique to Greece (as witness the statue of Il Commendatore in *Don Giovanni*), nor is the evidence overwhelming. When the Samian family group (62, 64) says 'Geneleos made us', this is not a proclamation of magic life but an explanatory statement similar to many epigrams about statues written in Hellenistic times. When Mantiklos (29), Nikandre (38) and Rhonbos (52) dedicate statues we do not know whether these are intended as likenesses of donors or are just *perikallea agalmata*, very beautiful presents. Unlike the Sumerian statues who say 'I am praying to my god on behalf of so-and-so', the Greek votives are not praying 'representatives' of the donors. In funerary sculpture the *stelae* and statues are called *mnema* ('memorial'), or *sema* ('sign') of the buried individual, but they may equally bear his name (iv, cf. 34) and thus represent him; it is, however, the ghost of the dead, not his statue, who rises from the grave and speaks in myths and legends.

Greece is the first country in which sculptors, painters and occasionally architects sign their works (34, 62). For the first time, society recognizes that an artist as well as a donor has claim to an undying share in his work before gods and men. As a matter of principle such a claim did not exist in

iv *Grave monument of brother and sister*
c. 540 B.C. marble 4·23 m.
New York, Metropolitan Museum

19

earlier cultures; here is the birth of artistic personality. On the basis of artists' signatures, later Greek writers constructed a sequence of schools, beginning, as the Greeks always did, with a *protos heuretes*, the 'inventor' of sculpture, Daedalus – apparently a real sculptor (*c.* 650 B.C.) who came from Crete, but whose personality was magnified by traits borrowed from legends of a craftsman-god known in Egypt, Phoenicia and probably in Minoan Crete. It is ironic that the vast destruction of Greek literature and art prevents us from writing in terms of individual sculptors the history of that sculpture which 'invented' the sculptor as an artistic personality.

The early (700–600 B.C.), so-called 'Orientalizing' phase was dominated by eager admiration of the wonders of the East. The most sophisticated examples are ivories, a material regarded with awe: did not Zeus replace Pelops' missing shoulder with one of ivory? Phoenician ivory-carvers were active at Ephesus (37) and probably elsewhere. Metal-work and metal-workers came from Phrygia, Urartu, Syria and Mesopotamia. The Greeks learned quickly. Already *c.* 750 B.C. a Greek made the ivory goddess from Dipylon (24).

With these *objets d'art* came stories of huge cities – 'Thebes with a hundred gates', and Babylon, on whose walls you could drive a chariot – and of huge temples decorated with monstrous creatures. Oriental myths and legends excited the Greek imagination; the Hellenes were always prone to recognize their own concepts in the beliefs of other lands. But admiration for the uncanny powers of Near Eastern and Egyptian monsters quickly passed. Just as in cosmogonic thought it is but a step from Hesiod's monstrous *Theogony* (*c.* 700 B.C.) to Thales' rationalized cosmos (*c.* 600 B.C.), so in architecture and sculpture the Greeks soon turned from fervent imaginings of 'Orientalizing' animals to creation of a rationalized, monumental order. As in geometry, so in sculpture, they found what they needed in Egypt.

The development of monumental sculpture was not uniform: a country divided into small city states developed regional schools. Their location was determined partly by the availability of marble, partly by the resources of patronage. Early trade with the Near East and superb marble quarries put Cycladic sculptors in an early lead (31, 38, 44, 48, 80, 87–8). Athens was almost equally favoured (iv, 35, 49–52, 54, 59, 67–9, 72, 93–4). A third important school arose in the mercantile centres of Miletos and Samos in Eastern Greece (42, 62–6, 70–1). The Eastern Greeks showed themselves venturesome and receptive to foreign stimuli; at the opposite pole, the schools of mainland Greece with Argos and Corinth in the lead (34, 61, 76–8), were strong on tectonic discipline and tradition. The Greeks in Italy largely followed this style (81, 92). In bronze, Samos, whose sailors went all the way to Spain for metal, was pre-eminent in the East (56, 58, 63); Argos (46), Corinth (57) and Sparta (90) in the West. Greek art historians maintain, and ancient inscriptions confirm, that this regionalism was counterbalanced by a surprising mobility of sculptors. The Athenian Endoios worked in Asia Minor, and Bathykles from Asia Minor created a colossal image in Sparta. Thus important innovations were diffused quickly.

The drama and freshness of the beginnings of Greek sculpture (650–580 B.C.) retain a never-ending fascination. From perfect imitations of Oriental ivories (24, 27–8), through the halting experiments to soften and enliven Geometric bronzes (26, 29, 36), the sculptors rise to the joyful, gigantic colossi of stone who take their proud places crowning the windswept promontories of Thasos and Sounion (33, 50). Then comes the time of reduction to measure, of humanization and elaboration (580–530 B.C.). Life-size or less, men and maidens smile friendly smiles and invite the admiration of the beauty of their bodies, hair-do's and garments (53–4, 57, 59, 62–8; III see p. 32). In a world often grim and always torn by strife, they proclaim that art will hold forever the youth and beauty cherished by the Archaic Age as the supreme present of the gods.

Late Archaic art (530–500 B.C.) runs into a Manneristic phase of delicate preciousness. Its subjects are close counterparts of boys and maidens celebrated in the courtly poems of Anacreon (III). This world of luxurious enjoyment of life was opposed by a new seriousness which we sense in the dark grandeur of the sayings of Herakleitos and in the traditions about the birth of Greek tragedy. It was a steady groundswell, but in sculpture its manifestations (51, 69, 95) appear rather suddenly. Like Expressionism and Abstract art before the First World War, Greek art prophesied, shortly before the event, a dramatic change. The new heroic attitude crystallized when Archaic Greece was shattered by that gigantic conflict with Persia which gave the Greeks a sense of playing a supreme drama on the stage of world history.

Early Classical sculpture

The years of Persian Wars spanned almost a generation. Between the Greek attack on Sardis and the Persian destruction of Miletus (494 B.C.) at the beginning, and the final battles at Plataeae (479 B.C.) and Mycale (477 B.C.) at the end, the Greeks had won the miraculous victories of Marathon (490 B.C.) and Salamis (480 B.C.). The feeling that a supreme and just divine order had upheld Hellas was all-pervasive, the sense of high calling omnipresent. The old Homeric ideal of a hero fighting for personal fame yielded to the ideal of the *polis* hero fighting for his country, for Hellas, and for a society of free human beings. 'Go, sons of Hellas, free your country, your children free, your wives, the altars of your native gods, and your ancestral tombs – all is now at stake' (Aeschylus, *Persians*). 'Great are the fallen at Thermopylae, nobly they ended, high their destination, beneath an altar laid, no more a tomb . . . where none with pity comes or lamentation, but praise and memory . . . a splendour of oblation no rust shall blot nor wreckful time consume' (Simonides). This high sublimity carries over into the view of the struggle against internal tyranny: 'Truly a great light dawned for the Athenians when Aristogeiton and Harmodios slew Hipparchos . . . and freed their native land. . . .' (composed already in 510 B.C.?).

Replacing a Late Archaic group (510 B.C.), the statues of the *Tyrannicides* by the Early Classic sculptor Kritios (477 B.C.) expressed the new ideal of the *polis* hero in plastic form (110). The same mood transformed the traditional athletic ideal: victory is a sign from on high, merited by trial and exertion: this is the spirit of the Delphic *Charioteer* (99, 102) and of Pindar's *Odes*. Divinity itself is purified from Homeric foibles and emerges as representing a lawful order on a cosmic scale.

Such was the ideological attitude of Early Classical times. On the political scene, the shift of power gave Athens leadership of Greece; while in the West, the kings and tyrants of Sicily achieved comparable glory by their victories over the Carthaginians (Himera, 480 B.C.) and the Etruscans (Cumae, 474 B.C.). From Eastern Greece leading philosophers and sculptors fled to this 'America of antiquity'.

The Classical revolution

All of this does not explain the revolution in sculpture which took place only once and only in Greece, from the Archaic concept in which a statue is constructed from outside by bringing together its separate views and has its limbs arranged to symbolize angular motion, to the Classical representation in which a statue is constructed 'from within' and appears to move organically and naturally. Basic for this transformation was the realization that motion in the human body is interrelated, that one part cannot move without affecting the others. The ultimate stimulus came from philosophy. The dynamistic definition of reality by Herakleitos with his examples of pull and counter-pull; the Pythagorean vision of a cosmos moving rhythmically in predestined geometric circles and spheres; the attempts of Parmenides and Zeno to analyze motion by 'stopping' it attest concern with the contrast of Being and Becoming. An intermediary between this abstract level of thought and the concreteness of sculpture was at hand in medicine, which just then emerged from magic into science. By the beginning of the fifth century, Greek physicians had a clear knowledge of the skeletal and major muscular systems. They must have begun to explain the motion of the body in terms of mechanics.

We do not know which sculptor or sculptors first adopted this discovery;

once made, it spread like wildfire and led a whole generation of pioneers to vigorous experiments with the human body in motion. The few original Greek statues give us just enough to see the general picture. In the beginning, the principle of motion from within was applied to the traditional *kouros* type (55). The sculptor of the 'Kritios' boy (51) observed 'the uneven distribution of weight which produces an opposition between a taut leg with knee held straight and a relaxed leg with the knee bent forward . . . but not the compensatory response in the upper body' (R. Carpenter) (51, 95). The Archaic lance-swinger became a 'starfish pattern' of outflowing motion in the *Zeus* of Artemisium (108–9).

Far bolder experimentation must have preceded the mastery of such complex poses as the pivoting *Hephaistos* (117) or Myron's wheeling *Discus-thrower* (114). To our great good fortune, a synopsis of these studies has survived in the metopes (111) and in the western pediment of the Temple of Zeus in Olympia (*c.* 460 B.C.). Its designer attempted to compose the two wings of the pediment in terms of two chains of interlocking motion of human and centauric bodies in varying degrees of stress and strain (119).

In their attempts to explore the effects of intensive motion and to relate them to anatomical observation, the Early Classical sculptors often went much farther than the following High Classical Age. The same pioneering intensity applies to the portrayal of emotion seen in grandiose Aeschylean mode.

The masters of Olympia contrast the quiet informal communication (98) with the violent clash of physical power (111) and, even more dramatically, 'the calm before the storm' in the east pediment (100) with the wild *mêlée* in the west (119). Set off against it in the centre is the towering, stern Apollo, who will uphold the right and punish hybris (96). This new concept of a divinity which without physical effort and immediate involvement 'by the thought of his mind' (Xenophanes) brings things to pass, found its expression in new statuary types. In a stance which implies a slow transition from rest to motion, the divinity reveals itself in aloof majesty. Goddesses, heroines and feminine devotees are thus portrayed in the austere 'peplos statues', in which the heavier Doric dress with its long vertical folds produces a tectonic, columnar effect (97, 143).

Bronze, with its fluid ductility, was the logical material to meet the need of Classical sculptors for fluid, flexible transitions. Henceforth, the finest realizations of stylistic ideals were usually in bronze (99, 109, 136, 151, 157); of many other masterly bronze statues we have only Roman copies in marble (107, 114–15).

Our sources and their limitations

This brings us to the problem of copies and to the larger problem of limits set to our knowledge of Classical and Hellenistic Greek sculpture. From the third century B.C. well into the second century A.D., the Romans carried thousands of Greek statues to Italy. Yet the guidebook to Greece written by Pausanias between A.D. 140 and 170 shows how much sculpture was still left in Greece. Some masterpieces were eventually transported by Constantine and others to Constantinople (A.D. 324); Phidias' *Promachos*, the *Knidian Aphrodite* (175), and a famous *Heracles* by Lysippos perished there. Most of the bronzes were melted down in Late Antiquity and Early Medieval times. Marble statues and reliefs were, after the fall of Rome (A.D. 487), steadily burned in lime-kilns, a practice which in some parts of the Mediterranean has persisted well into modern times. Nobody has ever tried to estimate the percentage extant, but the loss is staggering.

From Pausanias, from other ancient sources, of which the most important is the *Natural History* written by Pliny the Elder before A.D. 79, and from inscribed statue bases and other ancient inscriptions, we can reconstitute a history of Greek sculptors. Work on this verbal or literary history began in the Renaissance; until the nineteenth century it had a major influence upon the theory and practice of Western sculpture.

The great difficulty lies in linking this literary evidence with the relatively few surviving Greek originals. To give some illustrations: of all the Classical and Hellenistic statues selected for this book, only one, the *Victory* by Paionios (118) is accepted as an unchallenged original by a major master. Already less certain is the attribution of the sculptures from the Cave of Sperlonga to the Rhodian sculptors Hagesandros, Athanodoros and Polydoros (226, 238–40). Here the original Greek inscription was replaced by a Roman copy when the sculptures were taken to Italy. The famous *Laocoön* by the same sculptors (242) was recognized by Renaissance artists and scholars because Pliny (*Nat. Hist.* 36:37) said that it was in the palace of the Emperor Titus and showed 'Laocoön, his sons, and the marvellous intertwinings of the snakes'. Copies of the *Discus-thrower* by Myron (114–15) were identified because the essayist Lucian (*c.* A.D. 160), whose relatives were sculptors, gave an excellent description (*Philopseudes* 18). Other great masterpieces, the *Tyrannicides* by Kritios and Nesiotes (110) and the *Knidian Aphrodite* by Praxiteles (175) were recognized because they are shown on ancient coins of Athens and Knidos respectively.

But few ancient literary descriptions of famous works are specific enough and their use is beset with difficulties. Pausanias says that he saw a statue of Hermes by Praxiteles in the Temple of Hera at Olympia; many critics believe that the *Hermes* actually found there is a copy substituted by the Romans

(154–5). Most books on Greek sculpture state that the original of the *Meleager* was by Scopas (158). No ancient author says so. The attribution was made because of stylistic resemblance to the original Greek sculptures of the temple in Tegea – for which Scopas is mentioned as architect, not sculptor. The degree of probability sinks even lower in a case like the *Agias* from Delphi – a Greek original (156); he is given to Lysippos because the same family was represented in their home town of Pharsalus in a group made by Lysippos – of which only the inscription is known.

Roman copies

Matters are made more complicated by Roman copies, which we have already encountered in speaking of the *Tyrannicides* and Myron's *Discus-thrower* (110, 115). Already Hellenistic kings desired copies of famous Classical works, but these, like the *Athena* of the Pergamon Library (141), modelled on the *Athena Parthenos* of Phidias, were free paraphrases. In Roman times, in order to meet the enormous demand, copyists' workshops introduced (*c.* 100 B.C.) the use of copying machines which permitted much more precise imitation. Roman copies were largely made in marble, even when the originals were of wood, gold and ivory, or bronze. Translation into marble necessitated the addition of struts and supports, and the copyists often varied or even combined famous originals (283). Above all, in their actual execution these copies were works of their own times and show it. They can give us the overall composition; they can often give us reliable information on details. They cannot give us that unique and personal 'handwriting' of an artist, which is the ultimate touchstone for definition of artistic personality.

Some art historians accustomed to abundant and fully documented artists' *œuvres* have derided as chimerical all attempts to reconstitute the styles of famous Greek sculptors. In one sense this criticism is just; we have no work by the hand of Phidias or Polykleitos. We can, however, recognize the general stylistic character of a movement caused by a great sculptor. Just as we would have observed the existence of a Michelangelesque and a Raphael-esque style in sixteenth-century painting even if we did not have any information about these painters, so we can recognize a Parthenonian and a more 'constructivist' current in Greek sculpture of the fifth century B.C. We may call these stylistic groupings 'Phidian' and 'Polykleitan' as long as we are aware of the unknowns in this equation. Where the conventional reconstitution of famous Greek sculptors is likely to err is in assigning to great masters works done by lesser lights in their ambient; literary sources, original signatures inscribed on statue bases, and sculptors' names cited in payment accounts give us a far greater number of names than those to whom surviving sculptures have been attributed.

High Classical sculpture

The Early Classical phase passes gradually into that unique period which we might call 'Parthenonian' (*c.* 450–420 B.C.) but for the fact that some important aspects of this High Classical phase are not encompassed even by the miraculous ensemble of the Parthenon. It is the Age of Pericles (died 429 B.C.) and the great flowering of Athenian democracy which ends in the catastrophic war with Sparta (431–404 B.C.). It is the age of the heroic humanism of Sophocles (496–406 B.C.), but it is also the age in which the emotional and intellectual foundations of the Greek *polis* were undermined by sophism. The last quarter of the fifth century already belongs to another world. It is the time when the criticism of the divine and the emotional realism of a Euripides becomes effective, a time when Thucydides draws a scientific retrospective analysis of the glory and fall of Athens, and when the first historical and aesthetic criticism of literature and art appears. This is the great interest of the imaginary contest between Aeschylus and Euripides in *The frogs* of Aristophanes; critical discussion of painting and sculpture seem to be implied by Xenophon in his *Memoirs* and, less certainly, in some of the *Dialogues* of Plato.

The High Classical Age is the age of the unique balance: balance between simplicity and complexity of form; balance between reality and ideality; balance between body and soul; balance between the claim of the individual and glorification of the society; balance, ultimately, between the communal recognition of concrete divine powers in anthropomorphic form and the philosophic rationalization of the divine as a pantheistic abstraction. It was the last age in which a Greek society could genuinely envisage the Olympians (144) before they became remote beautiful legends or allegoric abstractions. The circle around Pericles which created the Parthenon held a highly intellectualized concept of the role of the divine and a lofty idea of the role of the *polis*. There is no reference to any specific god or goddess in the credo of Pericles, as formulated by Thucydides, which otherwise is virtually a programme for the Parthenon: 'the deeds of ancestors, who always inhabited this land and from whom we received a free State [metopes: battle against Amazons, centaurs] . . . our fathers who drove back the tide of war [metopes: Hellas against Asia=Fall of Troy]'; 'we are a democracy . . . in which a citizen is preferred to public service as reward of merit . . . games and sacrifices . . . a spirit of reverence pervades our public acts . . . we love the beautiful, we cultivate the mind . . . Athens is the school of Hellas . . . the individual Athenian in his own person . . . has the power of adapting himself to most varied forms of action with the utmost versatility and grace . . . Fix your eyes upon the greatness of Athens until you become filled with the love of her [the frieze].'

v *View of Parthenon from northwest*
c. 430 B.C.
Restoration drawing by Gorham
P. Stevens

Phidias was known as maker of divine images. As designer of the decoration of the Parthenon he emphasized that divine protection which Pericles omits. The two mighty pedimental compositions celebrated in a cosmic frame the Birth of Athena, who protected Athens, and her contest with Poseidon (122–32; v) which gave her undisputed possession of Athens. A brief reference to the Council of Zeus, who gave the Greeks victory over Asia, appeared in the metopes of the north side. The bold assertion that gods and ancestral heroes dwell with the Athenian democracy as equals was made in the frieze (103, 144). It was discreetly placed not to excite further the criticism of allies whose money was being used for the Periclean building programme; even in Athens the opposition accused Pericles of making out of Athens a whore laden with stolen jewels, and proceedings were instituted charging Phidias with embezzling some of the forty talents of sheet-gold which went to decorate the gold and ivory colossus of Athena Parthenos. Phidias had placed his signature on the *Athena Parthenos* (438 B.C.) (141–2) and on the *Zeus* of Olympia (432–420? B.C.) (139, 140). Such colossi required a workshop; we know the names of several collaborators and assistants. The mould for fashioning part of a fold of gold plate comes from his workshop in Olympia (vi). He must have made plastic models for the images. He may have done some work on the important parts of ivory – for instance the heads. But with the enormous tasks set by the two colossi and by the supervision of the entire building programme on the Acropolis, he cannot have carved any marble sculptures of the Parthenon.

27

No ancient source states that Phidias designed the sculptures of the Parthenon. The building accounts imply that the metopes were done by 440, the frieze by 438, the pediments between 437 and 432 B.C. The design of sculptures had to be done early. It is remarkable for the genius in the unified composition of major units; the occult symmetry and careful balancing of the long metopal sequences (112, 128), with the Capture of Troy using the same cosmic enframement by Night and Dawn as the east pediment; the incredible mastery in the symphony of the frieze rising to allegro of galloping horsemen and chariots (134), then ebbing to hymnic processional; the stupendous compositions of the pediments, in each of which an earth-shaking event spreads in waves which are both physical action and graduated emotional and psychological response (122–32); and finally the fertility and diversity of invention in varying figurative motifs – these attest a guiding hand. If the name of Phidias were not known, we would have to invent an anonymous 'Master Designer of the Parthenon Sculptures'.

vi *Mould from the workshop of Phidias* c. 430 B.C. terracotta L. 0·25 m. Olympia, Museum

In the Quattrocento we may distinguish artists concerned more with the new spiritual and ideological values and pioneers concerned more with the scientific rationalization of art; in High Classical sculpture, we find Phidias supplemented by Polykleitos: 'Beauty arises . . . in the commensurability [*sym-metria*] of the parts such as that of fingers to palm and wrist, and of these to the forearm, and of the forearm to upper arm . . . and in fact, of everything to everything else, just as is written in the *Kanon* of Polykleitos. For having taught us the proportions of the body . . . Polykleitos made a statue according to the tenets of his treatise and called the statue, like the book, the "Kanon".' This fragment of Polykleitos' book is cited by the physician Galen (*c.* A.D. 130–*c.* 200) after the Stoic philosopher Chrysippus (280–207 B.C.). It poses difficult questions about the exact nature of the system of proportions used by Polykleitos.[1] It leaves no doubt about his rationalistic attitude towards sculpture.

Copies (107) and reflections (106) of Polykleitos' canon show one unifying essential which the fragment omits: the slow curve of motion round which the figure is composed. Unconcern with immediate subject (the statue probably represented Achilles) does not mean absence of meaning. In their purity of form, timeless expression and slow unfolding in space, these statues harmonize with a divine rhythm which animates the entire world. Some such assumption was made in the geometric-musical universe of the Pythagoreans. From his geometric mathematical bias, it has been rightly conjectured that Polykleitos' attitude was shaped by contact with Pythagorean thought.

[1] Pollitt, p. 89.

Late Classical sculpture

'*The angry sunset*' (J. D. Beazley) of defeated Athens found few sculptors able to convey the anguish of her end (181). In an escapist, Manneristic slant, the grand Phidian images were manipulated towards sensuous delicacy (174) or were perpetuated as religious 'icons' to be adjusted to new allegorical concepts (170). Softened and made more approachable, the Phidian Zeus was transformed into the humane Asklepios, god of healing, in whom individuals rather than States put their trust (137).

The city states continued to fight their old feuds, first under the shadow of the Persians, then, under the growing thundercloud of Macedon; individuals withdrew into the family group whose living and whose dead are united forever in beautiful intimacy. This is the great age of the Attic grave *stele* (149, 160).

Few major projects of building were undertaken; the major challenges and rewards lay in the borderlands and beyond the frontiers. Already *c.* 400 B.C. a ruler in wild and mountainous Lycia commissioned Greek sculptors to decorate a monument second only to the Parthenon in the number of figures (133). About 350 B.C. the ambitious dynasty of Hecatomnidae of Caria culminated their building programme by inviting four famous Greek sculptors to adorn the funerary temple to Mausolos which became one of the 'Seven Wonders of the World'. In far-away Phoenicia, satraps of Sidon commissioned from Greek sculptors a series of sarcophagi for several generations (*c.* 450–320 B.C.; 222). Nevertheless, in philosophy and painting, Athens remained the School of Hellas; of the new generation of sculptors (*c.* 370–330 B.C.) who formulated the Late Classical ideals, Silanion (167–9), Praxiteles (154–5, 175), and Leochares (173) were Athenians. Others came from traditional centres of sculpture, Scopas (158, 182) from the marble island of Paros, Lysippos from Sicyon, but they travelled widely.

Marble knew its last refinement in the school of Praxiteles, whose famous *Knidian Aphrodite* (175) was of marble. The stone was tenderly modelled to suggest general softness and purity, yet without trespassing into the realm of detailed illusion (177, 180). The effect was made more naturalistic by painting in a colour scheme which favoured pastel hues and imitated optical effects such as highlights in the eyes. The sarcophagus of Abdalonymos (VI, *see* pp. 40–1) has preserved something of this evanescent colouration.

Late Classical sculpture (*c.* 400–330 B.C.) is classical because it retains the emphasis on generic life, on harmonious relation of body and soul, a belief in rational construction of artistic form, in preponderance of rhythm and proportion over naturalistic observation. But its artistic forms are far more complex and its scope much more diversified than that of High Classical art.

Its sculptors concern themselves with casual, relaxed play, with passion and defiance, with carefully specified states of body and soul.

In men-loving Archaic and Classical Greece, the male ideal influenced the rendering of the female. Now Praxiteles rediscovered the Eternal Woman on a new plane: he invented the Nude. He may have had a precursor in the painter Zeuxis (active *c.* 420–380 B.C.). When Zeuxis proposed to paint a picture of Helen for the Temple of Hera, he asked the people of Kroton to show him their most beautiful virgins. They immediately took him to the gymnasium and showed him their boys, saying he could imagine the beauty of their sisters. Zeuxis would not be side-tracked. Thereupon in a revolutionary move 'by resolution of the public council, Zeuxis was empowered to choose . . .' and selected five maidens '. . . for he did not believe he could find . . . in one body all the things he looked for in beauty' (Cicero, *De Inventione* 2:1). Clearly, earlier sculptors and painters had studied not specific models in a studio but boys at exercise – Myron's *Discus-thrower* (114) is probably the result of such practice; the study of nude female models was still unusual; and Late Classical artists thought a 'studio model' essential. But Praxiteles was not out to catalogue the charms of his mistress Phryne. Revealed in unselfconscious denouement, his *Aphrodite* (175) shares with other 'Praxitelean' works a dreamy remoteness isolating her from the spectator. In spite of direct appeal to the senses, she 'remains an ideal creation complying with abstract harmonies of art' (Sir Kenneth Clark). The discovery of femininity was not limited to the nude. Great goddesses are young mothers, grave, gracious, and understanding (172–3); young girls have a becoming adolescent seriousness which makes their delicate charm more charming (177–8, 180). The passionate creations of the 'Scopasian' current are the manifestations of a heroic dynamism, not models which are observed in action (158, 182).

It is in works reflecting a style probably originated by long-lived Lysippos (active 370?–300? B.C.) that a dichotomy of body and soul is first adumbrated (156, 160, 165). They show too a new canon 'making the head smaller . . . and the bodies slenderer' (Pliny, *Nat. Hist.* 34:61).

Observation of the individual was only incidental for Archaic art (34, 64, 75, 93–4); an inscription sufficed for identification. The Classical Age became concerned with the problem of the outstanding, powerful individual and his relation to society. A purely political reason, fear of tyranny, made individualized statues of living people suspect as arrogant claims of individual superiority. From 487 to 417 B.C., Athenians regularly voted to banish individuals who might prove too powerful. The end of this 'ostracism' coincides with first notices of portraits of living people. But forbidden fruit was sweet: Phidias was accused of representing recognizably himself (153) on the shield of the sacred image of Athena. What a shock for conservative Athenians to see the Persian Tissaphernes replace Athena's head on coins by his own quite recognizable likeness (162; 412 B.C.)! The Late Classical Age was certainly capable of detailed, convincing portraiture (169), but the hesitation to probe too deeply remained. The quality for which an individual claimed attention (161, 165, 167–9) prevailed over the 'uniqueness' of personality. Theophrastus' (c. 370–285 B.C.) *Charakteres* describes types, not individuals; and the Greek theatre never discarded the mask.

Radiation to periphery: Archaic, Classical and Etruscan sculpture

Already in the Late Archaic period Ionian Greeks worked in Oriental style in the palaces of Persian kings at Susa. Booty from Greece in Persepolis included Greek statues. It has been thought that the beautiful statue of the so-called Penelope type (217) might be the work of Telephanes, who 'offered his services to the workshops of Xerxes and Darius' (Pliny 34:68). During the fourth century Greek goldsmiths worked in Greek style on native themes for the Iranian Scythians in southern Russia (218–19). Greek influence was felt in the formation of Early Celtic style and reached into Iberian Spain (216).

The most amazing conversion to Greek art was that of the Etruscans (c. 800–50 B.C.), a people of non-Indo-European tongue, whose seafaring city states controlled the metal-rich Toscana and battled the Greeks in Italy until both Greeks and Etruscans were overcome by Rome. In the beginning

ii *Model of an Etruscan temple c.* 500 B.C. plaster
Rome, University, Istituto di Archeologia

(*c.* 750–650 B.C.), Etruscan sculpture stands between Geometric Greece and Iron Age Europe. Little bronze puppets expressively depict strange rituals and beliefs (189); and there is direct contact with the Near East in imports (191–2) and imitations (190). From the beginnings of the monumental style of Greek sculpture (*c.* 650 B.C.) Etruria becomes a faithful follower of Greece, but Etruscan imitation is often creative variation. Etruscan sculptors range from experiments in abstract geometry to detailed descriptive realism (211, 215), and from board-like 'Orientalizing' images (195) to full-bodied furies (208).

The favoured materials are the pliable terracotta and the native stones—tufa, limestone, alabaster, which are much more roughly treated than marble in Greece. Curiously, the Etruscans never exploited the Carrara quarries. With abundant supplies of the *Catena Metallifera*, Etruscans were renowned for their bronze-work. The Romans paid them a backhanded compliment by carrying two thousand bronze statues away from Volsinii. The best Etruscan Archaic sculpture (600–450 B.C.) is energetic in a joyfully earthy way; the famous *Apollo* of Veii is a picture of unholy glee (197). The later period (450–50 B.C.), the time of decline, dwells on passive or troubled moods (202–3, 209–13).

Dictated partly by their rituals, which called for observation of the skies, the Tuscan temples with their deep porches and heavy proportions were laden with painted and sculptured terracotta decoration (vii). Their designers used such Baroque effects as life-size statues acting out a mythological scene along the ridge-beam (198–9; IV).

Not being interested in rational science, the Etruscans never mastered the intellectual premises of Classical art. They caught its general appearance but not the motivation of its statuary types, not the calculated proportions nor the scientific study of movement (compare the Etruscan *Tinia*, 200, with *Hephaistos*, 117; or the gigantomachy, 198, with the Olympian sculptures, 111, 119). Well into the Late Classical Age they were apt to retain Archaic stylistic formulae, as in the patterning of the details on the famous *Chimaera* of Arezzo (201). The emotionalism of Hellenistic art was more to their liking. In the midst of depressing mass production of sarcophagi and funerary urns in Tarquinia, Chiusi, Volterra and Perugia, there occur striking characterizations which resemble Renaissance portraits (206, 210–11).

Without indulging in a mystique concerning survival of racial strains, one cannot help feeling that the Etruscan sculptors anticipated something of the fusion of Classicism and Realism which is characteristic of the Early Renaissance. Ruins of their architecture and art contributed to the mood and ambience in which the sculptors of the fifteenth century moved and worked.[1]

[1] Michelangelo is supposed to have drawn at least one Etruscan tomb painting.

Hellenistic sculpture

Lysippos as well as Leochares (active 370–320 B.C.) served as court sculptors to Alexander the Great (336–323 B.C.). The great conqueror exploded the boundaries of the Greek world and carried Hellenism into Egypt, Mesopotamia, Central Asia and India. His personal impact upon the artists he selected must have been overwhelming. The type of divinely inspired superman-ruler created for Alexander (220–1, 223) set a major theme for the new age, in which supermen contended for vast empires in Europe, Africa and Asia.

The shift of major patronage from city states to potentates broke up the relatively homogeneous high level of sculptural competence which had prevailed in the Classical period. Henceforth, international leaders and local practitioners tended to work on different levels. The sociological cleavage is curiously reflected in a Hellenistic theory preserved by Vitruvius (*On Architecture* 3, preface 2): artists become famous by the execution of works for great states or kings or citizens of rank; others of equal ability (among them Boedas, 247) are unremembered because they executed works for citizens of low station.

What little we have of great Hellenistic original sculpture indicates that artistic leadership centred in western Asia Minor and Rhodes rather than in the large new capitals of Antioch (Syria) and Alexandria (Egypt). Hellenism was the great age of exploration of nature by the Greek sciences. In most Hellenistic philosophies, the world theoretically remained divine, but the emphasis was on nature; the common lot of mankind was emphasized— '*Homo sum: nihil humanum a me alienum puto*' ('Nothing human is foreign to me'—Terence). Art responded by enlarging its thematic scope, from infants (253, 255) to skeletons (251), from grotesques (252) to noble savages (266), from pathos and passion (236–42) to relaxed sleep (244, 253).

The important shift was from the permanent 'ideal' reality to acceptance of immediate reality, of time and place as seen in nature. Not only do we hear of anatomical studies and use of casts, but the reality of specific setting is acknowledged. In relief, the 'ideal' impenetrable background, which only began to suggest emptiness in the reliefs of the Mausoleum (185), is more clearly sensed as 'air' even when obscured by unrhythmic massing of bodies, as on the sarcophagus of Abdalonymos (222; VI). In the reliefs of the altar of Pergamon, space is a flexible semi-optical substance out of which and into which bodies appear and disappear (236–7). The existence of specific landscape is acknowledged in the relief of Archelaos (269). More striking is the direct manipulation of setting for the *Victory of Samothrace* (viii), whose ship was sailing through a pool with real water. Similar effects including waterworks were probably employed in the original Greek as well as in the

Etruscan
VULCA?
Goddess and child c. 500 B.C.
Rome, Museo di Villa Giulia

33

later Roman location of the *Odyssey* scenes of Sperlonga (238–9). Yet no Hellenistic artist would have attempted the startling immediacy of Rodin's *The burghers of Calais*. The spectator may suffer with Laocoön; he cannot enter into the closely defined group (242). A line is still drawn between the sculpture and the beholder.

An intuition which Greek sculpture never gave up was the sense of a vital force, of a *vis vitalis*, and of a general ethos that makes even the most detailed portraits, even sick people and skeletons, typical. It is only when Greek culture had nothing new to say and sculptors started to imitate their own past that this vitality subsides.

In the complete picture of Early Hellenistic sculpture (330–250 B.C.), one movement initiated by Alexander (222, 224) preludes and probably leads directly to the rise of 'Hellenistic Baroque', whose spiralling dynamism dominates from 250 to 150 B.C. and ebbs into the first century. Its centres were the consciously Hellenic kingdom of Pergamon (272–133 B.C.) and the great maritime republic of Rhodes (229, 232–44, 269–70). Parallel rather than preceding is a movement whose exponents are consciously anti-Classic, which has been compared to modern Expressionism in form and spirit. Such works as Eutychides' *Tyche of Antioch* (227) are formal explorations of the new 'real' space and pyramidal composition. The term 'Rococo current' (*c.* 250–100 B.C.) indicates the range of erotic and Dionysian subject-matter, of urban admiration of 'nature's children', of infants, satyrs, maenads, and the delight in sensuous delicacy (253–8, 260, 268). This 'Rococo' approach gains dominance in the last creative phase of Hellenistic sculpture (150–100 B.C.).

Hellenistic Classicism

An art historian with a Classicistic bias cited by Pliny wrote that art stopped in 293 and revived in 156 B.C. We may be inclined to reverse that judgement. It is about the middle of the second century B.C. that retrospective admiration (141) begins to supersede creative impulses. A curious inventory of the first still largely 'sub-Baroque' phase is provided by a ship's cargo of sculpture which sank off Tunis *c.* 100 B.C.; its final, coldly mechanical phase of mass production of copies by another which went down in the Piraeus *c.* A.D. 150 (113). As the Romans sacked Syracuse (211 B.C.), Tarentum (209 B.C.), Pella (168 B.C.), Corinth (146 B.C.) and Athens (86 B.C.); as wars against the self-appointed liberator of Greece, Mithridates VI (88–63 B.C.), devastated Asia Minor and the Greek Islands; as civil strife in Rome and the cupidity of Roman governors drained Greece, Asia Minor and Sicily of their wealth and their art, sculpture in Greece declined. Many Hellenistic sculptors entered the service of Rome (245, 283).

viii PYTHOKRITOS OF RHODES *Nike* (*Victory of Samothrace*) *c.* 19 B.C. marble 2·75 m. Paris, Louvre

Roman sculpture

The conversion of Rome to Greek art and culture was a long process. In her early (*c.* 750–200 B.C.) days, Rome lived with Etruscan art. As she moved to conquer the Mediterranean (*c.* 270–31 B.C.) she first plundered, then fostered Greek sculpture. While architecture was recognized as the art of State authority, sculpture remained in a social penumbra: 'Others [Greeks, not Romans] shall draw breathing images from bronze and carve living faces out of marble', sang Virgil (*Aeneid*). Nevertheless, Virgil's patron Augustus set Late Hellenistic sculptors to the task of immortalizing the Empire he had created (287–8, 290–3).

To honour the leader of the Roman State and his family; to advertise the aims of the rulers with elaborate allegory and to recount the deeds of the Romans; to pay proper deference to traditional and now Hellenized gods, with accent on the ritual, these were henceforth the tasks of sculpture. Concern with funerary monuments, an obsession with the Etruscans, was strong with the Romans. In addition, the cultured Roman used sculpture for the adornment of his private life (VII, VIII). Old masters were collected, admired and imitated; contemporary sculptors disdained but given abundant employment. In the second and third centuries A.D. this output reached staggering proportions. Wealthy provincials competed with each other in adorning their cities; and each major architectural unit served for displays of sculpture (ix). Innumerable statues to all sorts of benefactors were erected, a habit begun by Hellenistic cities and assiduously continued in the Roman world.

Of the organization of this sculptural industry we have as yet a very inadequate notion. We know almost nothing of the leading sculptors. Some light on the history of one important workshop comes from the 'sculptors' city' of Aphrodisias in western Asia Minor, many of whose sons signed their work. As one of them says in his epitaph, they wandered through 'the cities of many men' (*Odyssey*) to Greece, North Africa, even to Hadrian's Imperial Villa in Tivoli. Literary sources and signatures show that it was an honour to have learned sculpture in Athens, which remained a great centre of copying and Classicism (113, 142) until overrun by Herulians (A.D. 263). Of the many workshops of Rome we have little information except from the sculptures themselves.

One should not think that a people who numbered their children – *Primus, Secundus*, and so on to *Decimus* – could be individualists; but by the time Hellenistic portraiture had become known in Rome the struggle between powerful individuals dominated the scene. Under the Late Republic (*c.* 100–31 B.C.) the Romans' comprehension of the uniqueness of the individual is of the same order as their sense of historical fact – a careful sober report of

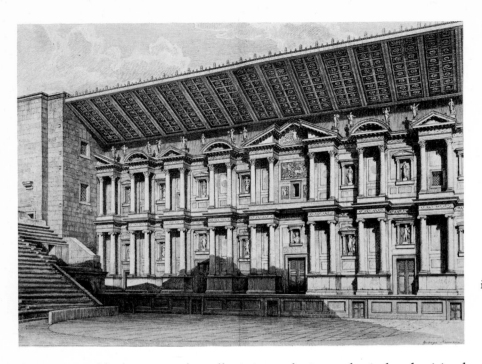

ix *Stage building with statues, Aspendos* c. A.D. 160–80 limestone, marble, granite, 22·6 m.
Restoration drawing by George Niemann

the ascertainable (280–1, 284). Hellenistic emphasis on physical and spiritual vitality added a dimension of depth (282, 289); but the synthesis is Roman. It is Roman, not Greek, portraits which Western European tradition accepted as definition of recognizable portraiture. The Roman individualizing trend prevailed time and again over the recurrent waves of Hellenic typification. The first of these came when Augustus (31 B.C.–A.D. 14) sought by conscious use of Classical form to attain for regenerated Romans the desired ideality of morals and spirit (285, 287, 293); it became a standard for the Julio-Claudian family and their subjects. Classicism under Hadrian bore the imprint of the complex and elusive intellect and emotional sensuousness of the Emperor (300, 302). The third Classicism, under Constantine and his successors, sought to use the distant glory of Classical form to bestow upon the new Christian ruler a beauty reflecting divine grace (318, 345). In varying ways all were tinged by the Roman sense for 'truth before beauty'.

Roman realism had a conscious revival as mirror of traditional Roman virtues under the Flavians and Trajan (c. A.D. 69–117). It reached a great psychological refinement in the times of stress beginning with the Emperor Marcus (A.D. 161–80) and continuing through most of the third century (308, 311, 315–16, 320). Even within the new un-Classical delineation of personality as a spiritual entity, as a 'soul portrait' (c. A.D. 260), the Roman observation of distinctive physical traits provided the individualizing touch (314, 319, 344, 346).

Posters made to show the Roman people what their generals and armies had accomplished, the so-called 'triumphal paintings', were the root of a news reporter's concept of history. They were supplemented by a sculptured record of the triumph. An early Augustan example (20 B.C.) enumerates in small, evenly spaced groups and figures the major features of a triumphal procession (292). On the famous *Altar of Augustan Peace* (13–9 B.C.) artists from Athens handle with great tact and varying success the difficult assignment of reshaping the procession of Athenian democracy on the Parthenon into a more specific, historical image of the Roman State under Augustus (290–1, 293, cf. 103). The Classical theme of the victorious charioteer (99) is evoked and Hellenistic paintings used as models for massed composition and high overhead space in the Arch of Titus (A.D. 81) (295, 296).

The 'book scroll in marble' rolled round the Column of Trajan (297) is the most clearly Roman achievement. The Parthenon frieze and the gigantomachy of Pergamon could be viewed consecutively by a perambulant spectator. The designer of the Arch of Titus strove to give to the spectator the illusion that he was looking at the Triumph of A.D. 71 as he entered the passageway of the arch. The 'reader' of Trajan's Column would have to ascend alternately to the floors of two libraries between which it stood if he wanted to 'read' its story. Finished in an incredibly short time (A.D. 106–13) the column presents in a hundred and fifty scenes, with some two thousand five hundred figures, an epic account of the Roman conquest of Dacia, based on the emperor's commentaries and the field sketches of the engineering corps. Carried out in fairly flat relief, its groups and motifs draw freely on Hellenistic paintings and reliefs, but place them in specific architectural and landscape settings. The report of Trajan, like that of Caesar's *Gallic Wars*, builds up step by step, by carefully chosen episodes, the image of the irresistible Roman army and its omnipresent leader.

The continuous narration of Trajan's Column is resumed on the Column of Marcus in a very different style and spirit. In an anti-Classical Expressionism brutalized puppets clash, torture and suffer in the bitter grip of war (307). Hieratic frontality appears in the reliefs of the Arch of Severus in his African home town, Lepcis (A.D. 203); abstract signification ('harmony in the Imperial family') prevails over naturalistic action (310). The style of Expressionistic squat figures culminates on the Arch of Constantine (A.D. 334–5) in the masses awaiting Imperial benefactions (335). Much more ambitious in the display of its many panels, the nearly contemporary (c. A.D. 300) Arch of Galerius at Thessaloniki merges elements of traditional Roman narration with the new emphasis on abstract programmatic objectives and the inherent virtues of divine rulers; the large decorative framework anticipates Byzantine ornamentalism (314).

The Roman lived in a world populated by sculpture. Rome and its vicinity was a vast museum where masterpieces of Greek sculpture of all ages could be seen, as well as myriad copies (299). In Rome alone three thousand seven hundred and eighty-five bronze statues were counted in the fourth century A.D. Without straining their own imagination Roman sculptors could readily pick types of bodies of gods and heroes to celebrate the emperors and empresses (282–4, 287, 300, 303, 311) and to eulogize patrons of lesser stature; these sculptural 'quotations' present a close parallel to the use of mythological similes in contemporary panegyrics and poems for birthdays, marriages, anniversaries and promotions.

While the traditional gods were perpetuated by images copying Greek types, the need to find adequate imagery for the native provincial (273, 305) and newly popular Oriental cults was among the few challenging tasks for sculpture. This was notably the case of the Iranian soldier-god Mithras, whose mysteries were carried by the army to the frontiers of the Empire (301).

During the Late Republic (c. 100–30 B.C.) sculptural output in Rome wavered between outrunners of Hellenistic Baroque (245–6), Hellenistic Classicism (283), and the more provincial Italo-Hellenistic (284) traditions. Julio-Claudian Classicism (c. 30 B.C.–A.D. 60) established a unified level of high skill (287) and a certain naturalistic vividness, which found its finest expression in floral ornaments (285–7, 288–9, 291). Already in this phase some use was made of optical effects of light and shade as a subsidiary device (290, cf. 271); these became a stylistic determinant under Nero and the Flavians (A.D. 54–96). With renewed admiration for Hellenistic Baroque (the Emperor Titus owned the *Laocoön*, and the sculptures of Sperlonga were perhaps installed under Domitian) came a taste for motion and for deepened space, as seen in the reliefs of the Arch of Titus (294–6). Official Classicism, antiquarian under Domitian, factual under Trajan (A.D. 99–117), sensuously nostalgic under Hadrian (A.D. 117–38), obscured but did not interrupt the trend. This attempt to combine and contrast heightened visual appeal with Classical sculptural form was accompanied in the Hadrianic and Antonine era by sophisticated differentiation of textures, such as flesh and hair (300–2, 321). So well had the human figure been mastered by Late Hellenistic sculptors that it seemed to present no new challenges; by turning to the exploration of optical effects and texture, Roman sculptors began to drift away from the basic tenet of Classical sculpture – the rhythmic animation of the human figure as a whole. Where the Romans insisted on observation was portraiture; consequently it is the heads which are observed carefully and remain alive (309–10). Apparently the nude human figure was studied less and less. Casts were taking the place of nature; Lucian speaks of a statue of Hermes in the Agora as being always covered with pitch because of casts that were being taken by sculptors.

The optical trend reached its culmination under the Late Antonines and

Severans (c. A.D. 180–235); combined with a resurgence of Oriental linear-ism, it produced the 'negative' formula for rendering folds as deeply cut lines (310, cf. 317). Another manifestation was the use of a shadowy 'negative' background (331) to replace the Classic insistence on a clearly defined and visible background plane. Some artists simply eliminated the background by a vertical pile-up of figures (especially from c. A.D. 190 to 260) (312). A device of great importance for expression was the use of shadow, then of light and shadow, to render the pupils of the eyes.

The Severan period (c. A.D. 194–235) still retained the general semblance of tall lifelike proportions and outward motion; but shortly thereafter the Classic concept of the human body was rapidly and widely abandoned. Already on the base of the Column of Antoninus Pius (after A.D. 161) there had emerged on the highest level of Imperial art (306) a canon of squat unorganic figures in which the rhythm of the individual figure was no longer worked out in detail. Hitherto, such primitivism had only occurred in pro-vincial and folk art as the result of incomplete assimilation of the Classical form. This trend comes into greater prominence on the Column of Marcus (A.D. 180–93) (307). It becomes widely prevalent during the time when the Empire is shattered (A.D. 235–84). Its final phase is codified into an official Imperial style (314, 334) when the Empire is forcibly renewed by four rulers (Tetrarchs) (A.D. 284–305). Its basis of systematic composition is no longer representation of lifelike reality but abstract mapping of conceptual relations – not the real battle but divinely bestowed 'victoriousness' (cf. 312 with 314).

In this fundamental break some influence was exercised by the resurgence of native attitudes and tastes, as in the sculpture of Palmyra (328); the basic reason, however, was the devaluation of the human body and increasing emphasis upon the life of the spirit. Late Roman and Late Antique art show a complex series of oscillations between 'anti-Classical' and 'Classical' attitudes (e.g. 310 and 331; 337–9, 341), but even before the victory of Christianity the abstract, transcendental view of reality had been established.

Radiation to periphery:
Hellenistic and Roman sculpture

Under the aegis of Rome anthropomorphic Classical sculpture spread over three continents. The encounter with native artistic traditions, begun in Hellenistic times, continued on a vaster scale and with greater intensity. Central and western Germany, France, England, Spain and Portugal, Austria, Hungary and the Balkan countries began to produce figurative sculpture modelled more or less closely on Roman examples. Booty, presents and tribute carried the Classical message into unconquered Scandinavia

(275) and Eastern Europe. The intensity of Romanization is attested by the emergence of 'Romance' languages; yet native religious, emotional, and artistic predispositions asserted themselves. The incoherently abstracted 'Gallo-Roman' lion (326) is both more grotesque and ornamental than any Roman marble sculpture, the blind barbarian (322) more emotionally stirring than the conventional Roman barbarians copied from Hellenistic giants (241). Even if the thread of monumental anthropomorphic sculpture was broken in Western Europe during the Migration period (c. A.D. 400–700), the phenomenon of first 'premature exposure' had its effect as it had in Protohistoric Greece some fifteen hundred years before. In the East the soil had been prepared by the Seleucid Empire (c. 300–65 B.C.) and other more ephemeral Hellenistic States in Central Asia (263). About 250 B.C. the Mauryan king Asoka of India published his interpretation of Buddha's Law in philosophic Hellenistic Greek.[1] Stone sculpture on a monumental scale was introduced to Asoka's court by Greek-trained, if not actually Greek, sculptors. At his capital of Patna in Northern India an Indian pupil may have fashioned the torso (278), Indian in its softness, but clearly of Greek inspiration. The school of sculpture which flourished in the land of Gandhara (Afghanistan, Pakistan and North India) from the first to the fifth century A.D. has been described as 'Greco-Roman form and Indian iconography' (B. Rowland). Thus the equestrian Buddha makes his Great Renunciation in the type of the philosopher on the throne, Marcus Aurelius (308, 330). Indian trade for spices by sea and caravan trade with China through Central Asia overland brought Roman sculpture to Central and even Far Eastern Asia; the influence was sustained by the intermediate Near Eastern zone.

As the battleground between the Romans and first Parthians (248 B.C.–A.D. 223) then the Sassanian Persians (A.D. 224–636), the Near East had its artistic traditions broken by waves of Hellenistic and Roman art, but its artistic and ideological predilections gradually reasserted themselves. The earlier Parthian phase was more susceptible to Hellenism. After the great Parthian victory over the Romans at Carrhae (55 B.C.) the King viewed a performance of Euripides' *Bacchae* – in Greek. Works of purely Greek style signed by Greek artists (274) stand side by side with images in which not only the Oriental costume but the Oriental linearism (277) create a non-Classical impression. Despite the use of Roman figurative types, the nearly immutable (c. A.D. 50–270) highly patterned style of the caravan city of Palmyra (328) is based on such partial synthesis. There is perhaps no more peculiar fusion of East and West known than in the funerary sculptures of the kings of Commagene, Harran of the Bible, Kumaha of the Hittites

V Early Classical Greece
Three sileni c. 480 B.C.
New York, Norbert Schimmel
Collection

VI Hellenistic
Battle scene, detail of Sarcophagus o
Abdalonymos c. 320 B.C.
Istanbul, Archaeological Museum

VII Roman
Statue of Mars c. A.D. 70
Pompeii, Casa di Venere
(VI & VII *overleaf*)

[1] These inscriptions in Greek and Aramaic were found in 1958 and 1963 near Alexandropolis-Kandahar 'in the glacis which forms the transition between the crests of Hindukush and the plains of Indus'. D. Schlumberger, *Comptes rendus de l'Académie des Inscriptions*, 1966, 41; 1965, 126.

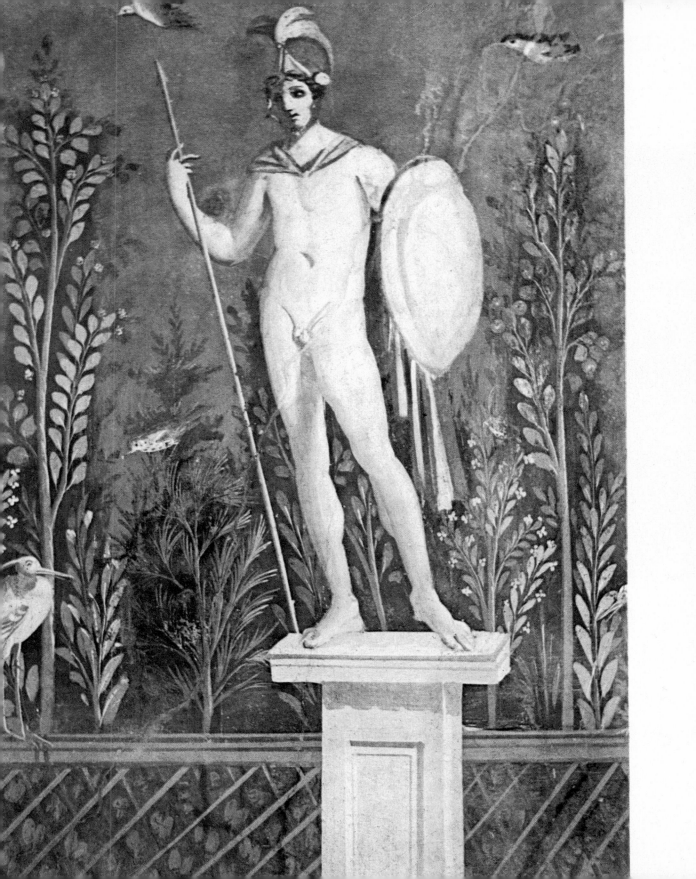

(276). In their inscriptions written in Greek these kings invoked Hittite, Iranian and Greek gods; in exact parallel, provincial Hellenistic sculpture provides the formal vehicle as the King in Oriental costume shakes hands with Heracles.

With its millennial tradition of divinely prescribed art, Egypt successfully resisted any real penetration by Hellenistic sculpture; Hellenistic (279) and Egyptian sculpture went side by side. The breakdown of Egyptian traditions came under the Romans. As supplier of Royal porphyry, Egypt had its brief moment of glory when Tetrarchic abstractionism first arrived: its most impressive monuments are porphyry sculptures made in Egypt (336). The victory of Greco-Roman tradition came just in time to give issue to semi-Christianized Coptic art. Strangely unlike the monolithic sculpture of Pharaonic Egypt, its ornamentalized creations weave bizarre chiaroscuro patterns out of inherited Greco-Roman mythology (333). In North Africa, from old prosperous Greek foundations (Cyrene, cf. 151) Roman urbanization carried Classical and Hellenistic sculpture as far as Atlantic Morocco. Some of the finest copies of Hellenistic and Roman portraits have been found in a third-century A.D. house at Volubilis (289), two hundred miles south of Gibraltar.

Late Antique sculpture

After the Peace of the Church (A.D. 312) the Roman Empire did not turn Christian overnight. High-level attempts to return it to paganism continued until the end of the fourth century A.D. The fourth century is very much a phase of transition. The end of ancient sculpture is more clearly marked by the Edicts of Theodosius I (c. A.D. 380) which caused the closing and destruction of pagan sanctuaries. Even before, barbarian raids had finished the large sculptors' workshops in mainland Greece and most of the provinces. In Rome, statuary in the round, at any rate, appears in much reduced quantity during the fourth century (317–18, 343, 345). In Western Asia Minor, at Aphrodisias, Ephesus and Constantinople (344, 346), the making of anthropomorphic sculpture of curiously uneven quality continued into the time of Justinian and perhaps longer; the last statues of emperors are attested for A.D. 711–13.[1] Figurative sculpture in relief was represented more abundantly and continuously by sarcophagi. Workshops for these existed in Rome (338–9), Northern Italy (337), Gaul and Spain; in the 'Sacred Fortress' of Ravenna (347) this tradition lasted into the eighth century. The anti-iconic trend limited stone sculpture in many regions to architectural, largely non-figurative decoration. Functions previously exercised by monumental

III Roman
HADRIAN
Aphrodite of Knidos in the Round Temple c. A.D. 121–38
Tivoli, Villa of Hadrian

[1] C. Mango, 'Antique Statuary and the Byzantine Beholder', *Dumbarton Oaks Papers*, 1963, is a vivid and enlightening account.

sculpture such as honouring of officials and offerings for religious purposes
were now assumed by the portable luxury objects, gold and silver ware and
ivories (341, 348) produced in the service of the imperial courts, and,
eventually, of the Church.

Early Christian sculpture

'Thou shalt not make unto thee a graven image'. This thunderous prohibition
stood in the way of any figured Christian art. The struggle of pure, transcendental monotheism against idolatry had agitated the Hebrews and erupted
in the Iconoclastic movement and during the Reformation. Yet so thoroughly
was Greco-Roman culture imbued with anthropomorphic imagery that if
its education was accepted, anthropomorphic imagery followed. As *Rhomaioi*
the Byzantines continued to portray emperors and acts of State; as *Hellenes*
they continued to depict Greek mythology (348).

The real issue was with cult images. The destruction of idols was a pious
deed, and once begun it became a characteristic activity of many a saint.
Because Classical idols were chiefly sculpture, sculpture was to many
Christians more suspect than painting. According to Epiphanius (Bishop of
Cyprus, A.D. 367–403), 'the fashioning of statues from moulded mud by
Terah' was a greater wickedness than the portrayal of idols in painting by
Serug.[1] This feeling prevailed in the Eastern Church after worship of images
was finally made canonical by the Second Council of Nicaea (A.D. 787).

Painted images of Christ were known to heretic Carpocratians by about
A.D. 150. Early Christian sculpture began almost innocently (A.D. 200),
probably in the lower social strata and perhaps with a desire to replace the
pagan decoration of commercially supplied sarcophagi and tomb paintings
with symbols which at least hinted at the Christian faith of the deceased. This
direct conversion of pagan motifs into general Christian symbols is seen on
the sarcophagus of La Gayole (*c.* A.D. 250) (331); its Zeus-like philosopher
and Hellenistic Good Shepherd were apparently adequate symbols of
Paradise.

The triumph of the Church and the supreme importance of a Christian
emperor were decisive for the brief flowering of Antique Christian sculpture.
Roman biographical sarcophagi which condensed a life into three or four
significant scenes were drawn upon for the first sculptured cycles of the life
and deeds of Christ (338). Late Roman imperial reliefs glorifying the
emperor as world ruler were immediate models for the Lord of Hosts; he
was shown as law-giver and true philosopher (339, 343), a simile frequently
used by Early Christian apologists.

Should He who suffered a humiliating death on the Cross be shown as

[1] E. Bevan, *Holy Images*, 1940, p. 52.

42

humble and despised, or in the ineffable beauty in which He will appear to the faithful? The master of the ivory relief (341), one of the earliest to show Christ crucified, may have thought of the humility of Christ, but in general the accent was on his beauty and glory, especially in the Greek East. Constantine, who did not object to being represented by a statue of Helios or Apollo Christianized by addition of a cross, and who carried so many Classical images to his new capital, encouraged the formal Classicism which prevailed well into the fifth century (336, 339–40). For a while it seemed as if the intensive spirituality of the new faith might bring new life to the well-worn Classical forms. Constantine's great colossus in Rome (318) was not only a compelling crystalline image of the new ruler by divine grace; its other parts show Classical clarity and exceptional 'Classical' skill in carving. An echo of the *Knidian Aphrodite* appears in the Eve of the sarcophagus of Junius Bassus (175, 340). The sarcophagus in S. Vitale (347), intentionally Classicistic, displays the pure 'neutral' background and stress on rhythm; but how uniform and abstract is the motion, how superficial the bodies if one looks back at the Classical reliefs (185).

Imperial images of other-worldly grandeur (344–5) and portraits of hypnotic spiritual intensity were still fashioned in plastic form during the fifth and sixth centuries (346). But the tide was going against sculpture. Monumental work of stone and bronze was expensive. It had derived its support from a highly organized and affluent society, now swept away by invasions and reduced by disease. Rome, which may have had up to a million inhabitants in the fourth century A.D., counted perhaps only twenty thousand in the seventh.

The Classical ideal had deified the human body; the Christians humiliated and mortified it. The Classical ideal was based on organic comprehension of the nude; nudity became sinful to Christianity. The Classical ideal saw the divine in the rhythm of nature; the Christian God was a miracle, worked miracles, and was above the laws of nature.

The number of sculptural monuments dwindled. An early medieval pilgrims' guide to Rome lists many arches and columns, but only three statues. In Constantinople some hundred bronzes had survived; the majority were melted down by the Latin Crusaders in 1204. A few were brought to Italy (344). The Heracles reliefs on the Golden Gate and the Serpent Column from Delphi were the sole survivors when the city fell to the Turks in 1453. Early Renaissance humanists lamented that only a half-dozen works of ancient sculpture were to be seen in Rome.

Those sculptures which survived during the Middle Ages underwent a curious metamorphosis. Because Early Christian Fathers had held that the images were inhabited by demons, attention centred on the magic capabilities of ancient sculptures. In 1204 the Constantinopolitans pulled down a great bronze *Athena* by Phidias; she was suspected of beckoning the attacking Crusaders into town. In the West, even the identity of ancient monuments was rapidly forgotten: *Marcus Aurelius* (308) became a knight who saved Rome. The colossal *Dioscuri* on Monte Cavallo, mistakenly inscribed under Constantine 'work of Praxiteles' and 'work of Phidias' respectively, were explained as two philosophers 'naked because all worldly knowledge is naked and open to their minds'. (*Mirabilia Urbis Romae.*)

The fundamental heritage of Classical sculpture, its anthropomorphic vocabulary and compositional syntax, was saved by media other than monumental sculpture: manuscripts, ivories, metal-work, gems. Some sculptures were re-used, as were the ancient reliefs in the Little Metropolitan Church, Athens, or the Roman sarcophagi in the Campo Santo, Pisa. Scattered though they were, they presented potential stimuli for revivals. Sculpture seems to have played no great role in the 'Carolingian Renaissance', but already, *c.* 1020, Bishop Bernward of Hildesheim, who had lived in Rome, was inspired to erect his triumphal column of Christ in clear recollection and emulation of the columns of Trajan and Marcus. The implied aesthetic appreciation became explicit when Henry, Bishop of Winchester, second brother of King Stephen, collected and exported pagan statues from Rome to England (1151). A little later another Englishman, Magister Gregorius, ran three miles to admire a *Venus*, possibly the '*Capitoline*' *Venus* (254), 'a living creature rather than a statue . . . of wonderful and inexplicably perfect workmanship'. Thus Classical sculpture was beginning to work a different kind of magic. In the 'Proto-Renaissance' in Italy and in the Romanesque in France, the newly awakening monumental sculpture of Europe had its first creative encounter with the Classical ideal.

NOTE: Where there is more than one illustration on a page the captions and pictures run from left to right and top to bottom.

THE FORERUNNERS

1 Neolithic Anatolia
Goddess and young god c. 5400 B.C.
Ankara, Hittite Museum

2 Early Bronze Age Greece
Phallic man c. 2500 B.C.
Athens, National Museum

3 Cycladic Islands
Female idol c. 2400 B.C.
Boston, Museum of Fine Arts

4 Cycladic Islands
Harpist c. 2000 B.C.
Athens, National Museum

Minoan Crete
Bull jumper 16th cent. B.C.
Heraklion, Archaeological Museum

Minoan Crete
Praying woman 16th cent. B.C.
Berlin, Staatliche Museen

Minoan Crete
Worshipping youth c. 1500 B.C.
New York, Walter C. Baker Collection

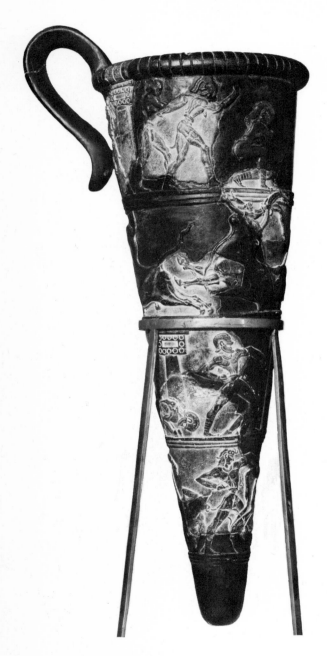

8 Minoan Crete
Boxing scene c. 1500 B.C.
Heraklion, Archaeological Museum

9 Minoan Crete
Sacred mountain 1500 B.C.
Heraklion, Archaeological Museum

10 Mycenaean Greece
Lion gate 13th cent. B
Mycenae

11 Minoan Crete?
Smiling youth 14th cent. B.C.
Athens, National Museum

2 Mycenaean Greece
Head of a king 16th cent. B.C.
Athens, National Museum

Cyprus
God with horned cap 12th cent. B.C.
Nicosia, Cyprus Museum

14 Cycladic-Minoan (Keos)
Female figure 1500 B.C.
Keos, Temple at Ayia Irini

15 Mycenaean Greece
Head of Poseidon? 12th cent. B.C.
Nauplion, Museum

GEOMETRIC
SCULPTURE
OF GREECE

16 *Stag* 'Protogeometric' 11th cent. B.C.
Athens, Kerameikos Museum

17 *Horse* 8th cent. B.C.
New York, Metropolitan Museum

8 *Deer and fawn* 750–700 B.C.
Boston, Museum of Fine Arts

9 *Dancing women* 8th cent. B.C.
Athens, National Museum

Warrior 8th cent. B.C.
New York, Metropolitan Museum

Charioteer 8th cent. B.C.
Olympia, Museum

22 Helmet-maker 680–650 B.C.
New York, Metropolitan Museum

23 Running man early 7th cent. B.C.
Paris, George Ortiz Collection

GREEK ARCHAIC
SCULPTURE

24 *Goddess or votary* c. 750–725 B.C.
Athens, National Museum

25 *Priestess* 570–550 B.C.
Istanbul, Archaeological Museum

26 *Apollo* c. 650 B.C.
Heraklion, Archaeological Museum

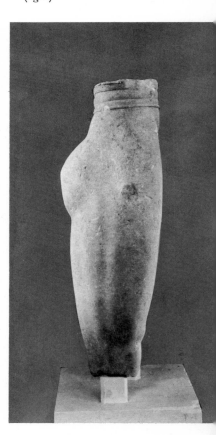

33 *Kriophoros c.* 600 B.C.
Thasos, Museum

34 (POLY?)MEDES OF ARGOS
Kleobis and Biton c. 590 B.C.
Delphi, Museum

38 *Nikandre c.* 640 B.C.
Athens, National Museum

Protome of lion c. 700 B.C.
Olympia, Museum

Lion waterspout c. 650 B.C.
Olympia, Museum

42 *Lion c.* 525–500 B.C.
Berlin, Staatliche Museen

41 *Lion guarding grave c.* 600 B.C.
Korkyra, Museum

43 *Lion*, view from back of 42

Lions at Sacred Lake c. 620 B.C.
Delos, Sacred Road

Gorgon mask c. 700 B.C.
Nauplion, Museum

Griffin c. 650 B.C.
New York, Walter C. Baker
Collection

7 *Sphinx* 625 B.C.
  Athens, Kerameikos Museum (*left*)

8 *Sphinx of the Naxians* 580 B.C.
  Delphi, Museum

49 *Funerary sphinx* 530 B.C.
  Boston, Museum of Fine Arts

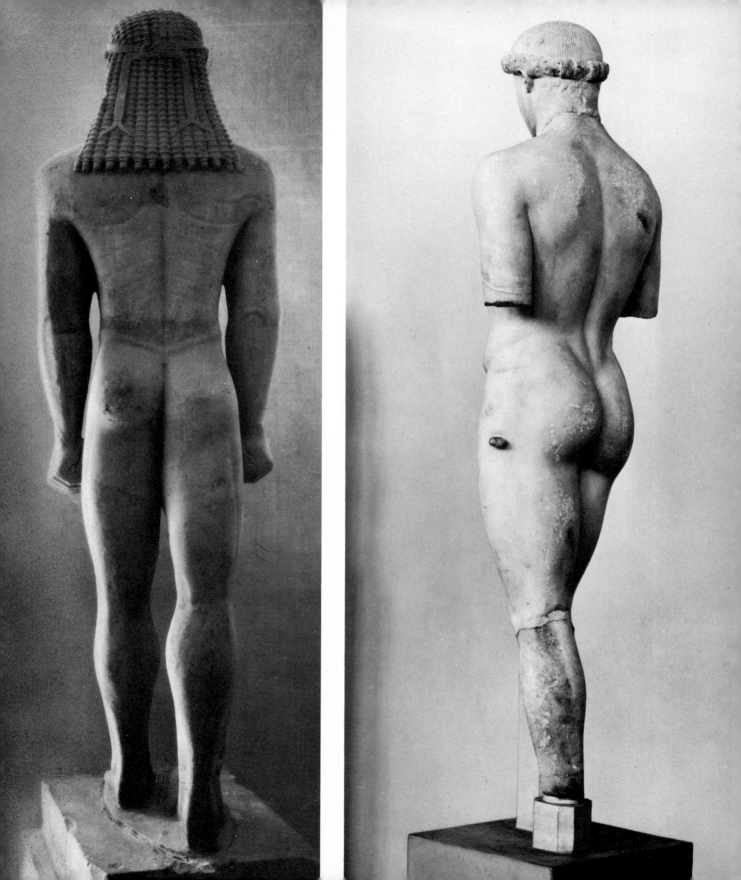

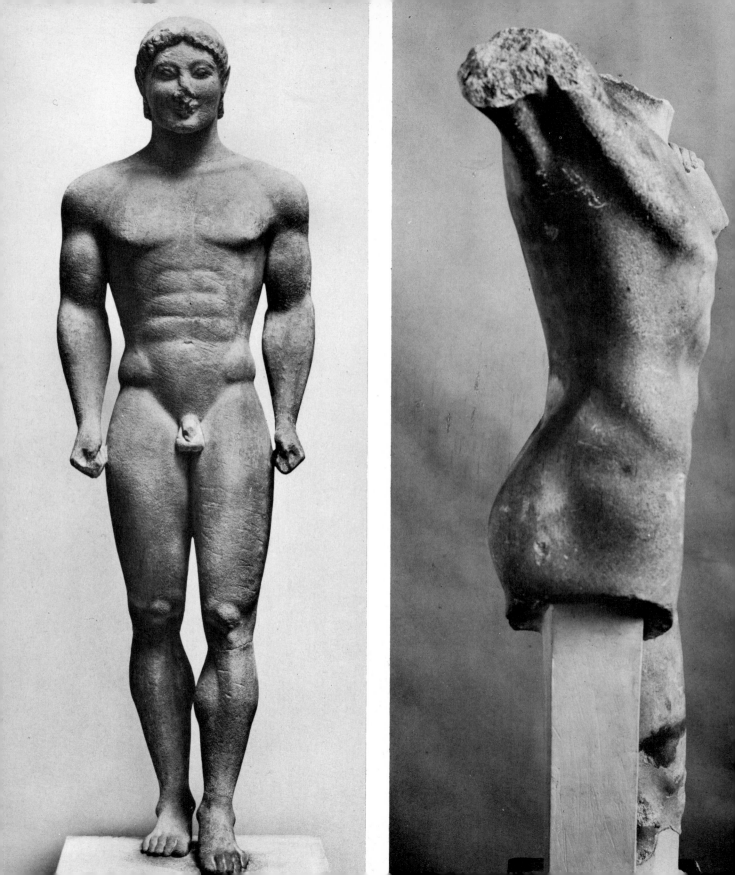

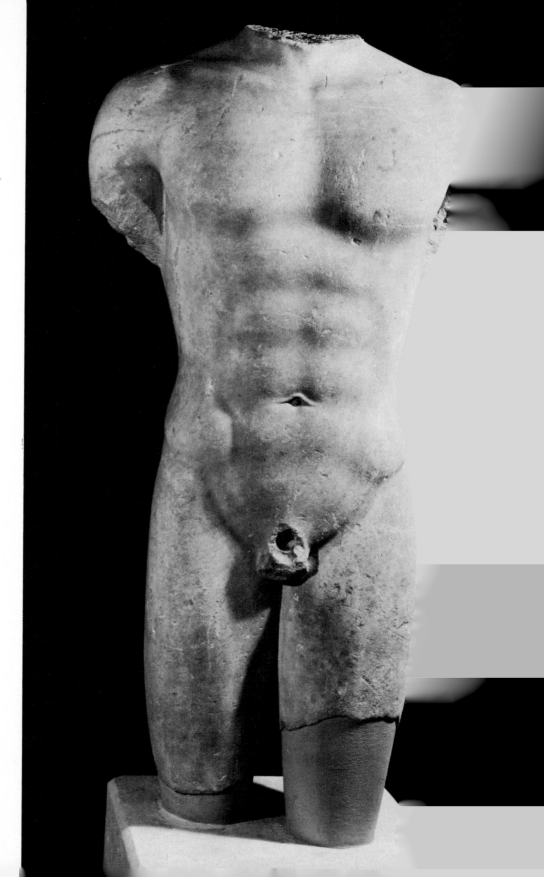

56 *Horseman*, detail of 58

57 *Horseman c.* 550 B.C.
Athens, National Museum

58 *Horseman* 530 B.C.
Vathy (Samos), Museum

59 'Rampin' horseman *c.* 560 B.C.
Paris, Louvre, and Athens, Acropolis
Museum

Horseman 560 B.C.
Manisa, Archaeological Museum

Basin supported by goddesses 620 B.C.
Corinth, Museum

GENELEOS
Family group c. 560 B.C.
Vathy (Samos), Museum

GREEK ARCHAIC

67 '*Peplos*' *kore* 540–530 B.C.
Athens, Acropolis Museum

68 *Head of the* '*Peplos*' *kore*, detail of (

69 *The 'Sphinx' kore c. 500 B.C.*
Athens, Acropolis Museum

Seated priestly ruler 570 B.C.
London, British Museum

71 *Aeakes?* 540 B.C.
Tigani, Museum

GREEK ARCHAIC

72 *Seated man* 530–520 B.C.
   Athens, Kerameikos Museum

73 *Proteus?* 550 B.C.
   Athens, Acropolis Museum

74 *Persephone?* 470 B.C.
   Berlin, Staatliche Museen

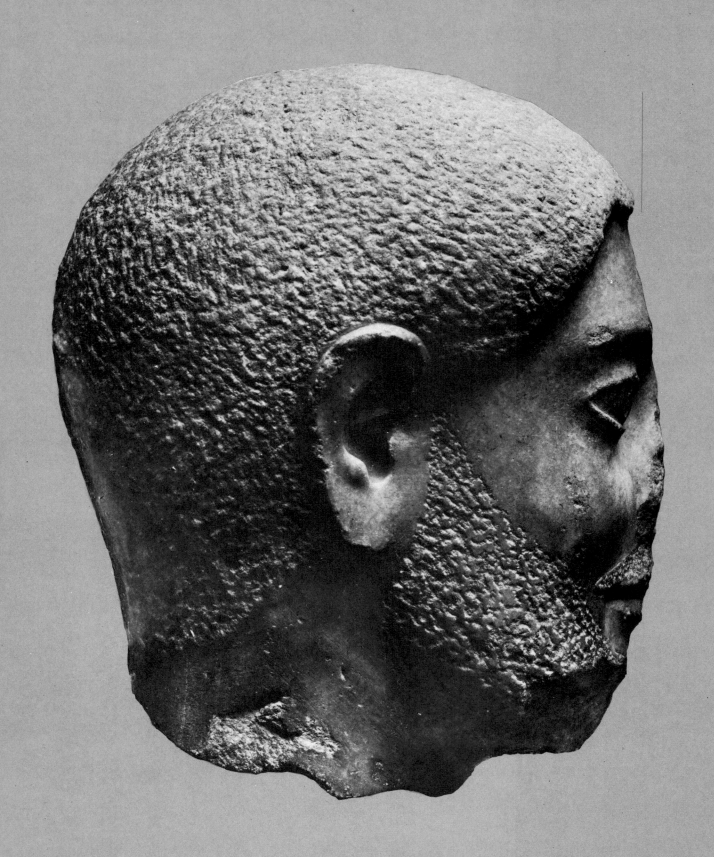

A portrait? 540–530 B.C.
Berlin, Staatliche Museen

Winged youth 650 B.C.
Athens, National Museum

Owl c. 650 B.C.
Paris, Louvre

78 *Gorgon from the Temple of Arten*
detail of 79

79 *West pediment, Temple of Artemis*
580 B.C.
Korkyra, Museum

Flying Victory (Nike) 550 B.C.
Athens, National Museum

81 *Gorgon* 560 B.C.
   Syracuse, Museo Archeologico

82 *The Trojan Horse* 675–650 B.C.
   Mykonos, Museum

83 *Dead man torn by vulture* 680 B.C.
   Athens, National Museum

Monument in form of Ionic temple 550 B.C.
Manisa, Museum

85 *Frieze of horsemen* 640 B.C.
Heraklion, Museum

86 *Heracles slaying centaurs* 540 B.C.
Boston, Museum of Fine Arts

Battle between Greeks and Trojans 530–525 B.C.
Delphi, Museum

Battle of gods (Heracles and Cybele) and giants
530–525 B.C.
Delphi, Museum

89 *Cybele's lions fighting giants*, detail of 88

91 *Warrior and chariot*, detail of 90

Heracles and the Kerkopes 560 B.C.
Paestum, Museum

Boxer 550 B.C.
Athens, Kerameikos Museum *(right)*

Child and mother's hand c. 530 B.C.
Athens, National Museum

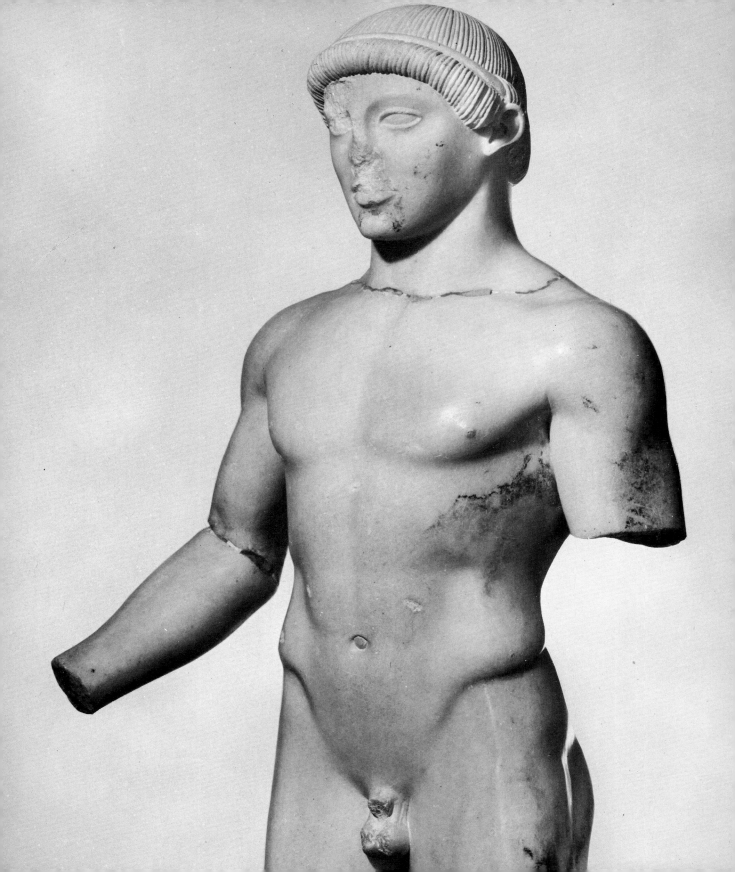

Youth (athletic victor?) c. 480 B.C.
Agrigento, Museo Civico

CLASSICAL
GREEK
SCULPTURE

Apollo 460 B.C.
Olympia, Museum

99 *Charioteer* 477 B.C.
Delphi, Museum

100 *Oinomaos and Sterope?* 460 B.C.
Olympia, Museum

I *Head of Athena*, detail of 98

2 *Head of the charioteer*, detail of 99

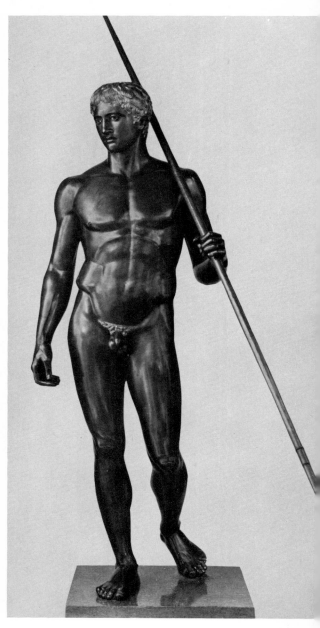

106 *Funerary stele of a warrior* 420 B.C.
Worcester, Mass., Art Museum

107 POLYKLEITOS
Doryphoros original *c.* 450 B.C.,
modern reconstruction
Munich, University

8 *Heracles c.* 500 B.C.
Athens, National Museum

109 *Zeus or Poseidon?* 460 B.C.
Athens, National Museum

110 KRITIOS and NESIOTES
   Aristogeiton (part of *Tyrannicide*
   group) original 477 B.C., Roma[n]
   copy
   Rome, Palazzo Conservatori

111 *Heracles and the Cretan bu[ll]*
   c. 460 B.C.
   Paris, Louvre, and Olympia,
   Museum

112 *Centaur triumphant* 442 B.C.
London, British Museum

113 *Greek and Amazon* original
438 B.C., Roman copy *c.* A.D. 15
Piraeus, Museum

114 MYRON
Discus-thrower original *c.* 440 B.
modern reconstruction
Rome, Museo Nazionale de
Terme

115 MYRON
Discus-thrower original *c.* 440 B.
Roman copy
Rome, Museo Nazionale de
Terme

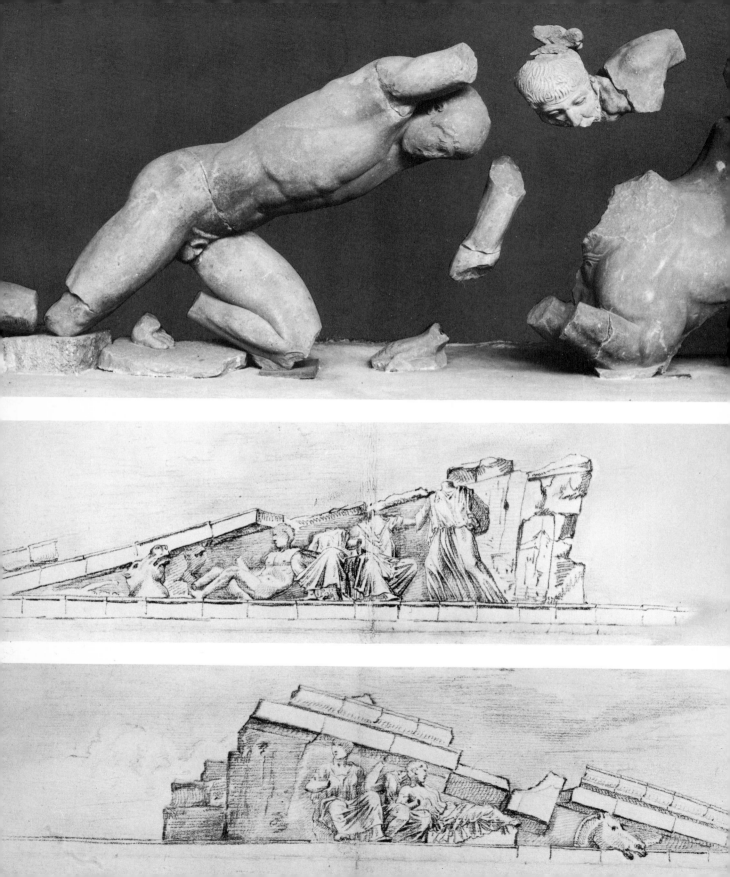

Youth battling a centaur c. 460 B.C.
Olympia, Museum

& 121 ANONYMOUS FLEMISH
DRAUGHTSMAN
East pediment of the Parthenon 1674
Paris, Bibliothèque Nationale

Head of Dionysos, detail of 123

Dionysos? 437–432 B.C.
London, British Museum

Demeter, Kore and messenger 437–432 B.C.
London, British Museum (*left*)

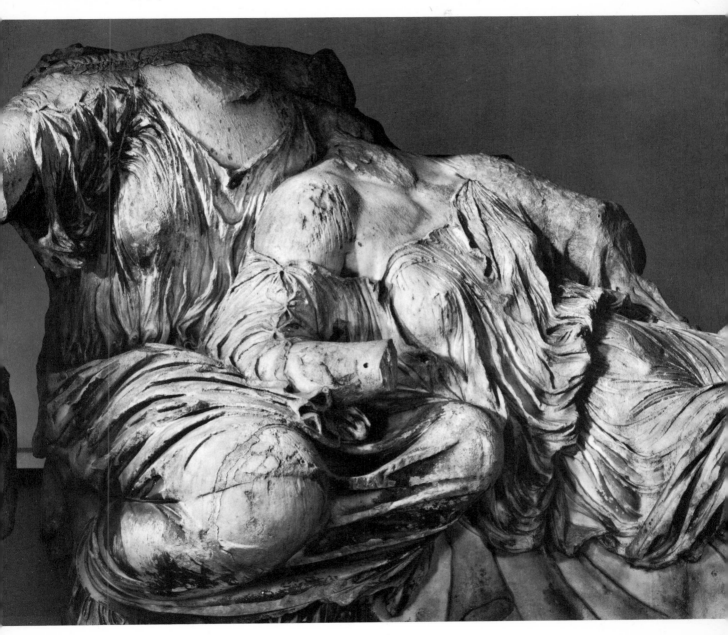

Hestia?, Dione?, Aphrodite 437–432 B.C.
London, British Museum

126 *Dione? and Aphrodite*, detail of 125

127 *Horse-head from Selene's chariot* 437–432 B
London, British Museum

128 *Northeast corner of the Parthenon*
Athens, Acropolis

129 *Kekrops and daughter*, detail of 1

130 *River god or hero?* 437–432 B.C.
London, British Museum

Kekrops and daughter 437–432 B.C.
Athens, west pediment, Parthenon

132 *Amphitrite* 437–432 B.C.
London, British Museum

Siege of Troy? c. 400 B.C.
Vienna, Kunsthistorisches Museum

Chariot c. 438 B.C.
London, British Museum

135 *Assembly of gods* c. 420 B.C.
Athens, Temple of Athena Nik
Acropolis

136 *Head of Apollo* 460–450 B.C.
London, British Museum

137 *Asklepios c.* 380 B.C.
Athens, National Museum
(*left*)

138 PHIDIAS
Head of Zeus of Olympia c. 430 B
on coin of Elis
Berlin, Staatliche Museen

139 PHIDIAS
Zeus of Olympia c. 430 B.C. on co
of Elis
Florence, Museo Archeologico

141 PHIDIAS
    Athena Parthenos Hellenistic cop
    c. 160 B.C.
    Berlin, Staatliche Museen (Perga
    mon Museum)

142 PHIDIAS
    Athena Parthenos original *c.* 438 B.C.
    Roman copy *c.* A.D. 130
    Athens, National Museum

143 *Aphrodite* 460–450 B.C.
    Cambridge, Mass., Fogg Art
    Museum, Harvard University
    (*far right*)

144 *Artemis* 438 B.C.
Athens, Acropolis Museum

145 *Head of a woman* 420–410 B.C.
Athens, National Museum

'*Caryatid' maiden* 420 B.C.
London, British Museum

147 *Caryatid*, Roman copy of *Erech-theum maiden* 10–4 B.C.
Rome, reconstructed in Loggia of
the Knights of Rhodes

148 *Erechtheum maiden*, copy
c. A.D. 125
Tivoli, Canopus, Hadrian's Villa

149 *Funerary stele of Ampharete* 420 B.
Athens, Kerameikos Museum

DEXAMENES OF CHIOS
Portrait of a man 420 B.C.
Boston, Museum of Fine Arts

151 *Arkesilas IV of Cyrene?* *c.* 450 B.C.
Cyrene, Museum

ΘΕΜΙΣΤΟΚΛΗΣ

Themistocles herm original
c. 450 B.C., Roman copy
Ostia, Museo Ostiense

Portrait of Phidias original 438 B.C.
Hellenistic copy
London, British Museum

LATE CLASSICAL
GREEK SCULPTURE

154 PRAXITELES?
Hermes and infant Dionysos c. 360
Olympia, Museum

155 PRAXITELES?
Hermes and infant Dionysos, quar[ter]
view from the back of 154

156 *Agias c.* 336 B.C.
Delphi, Museum

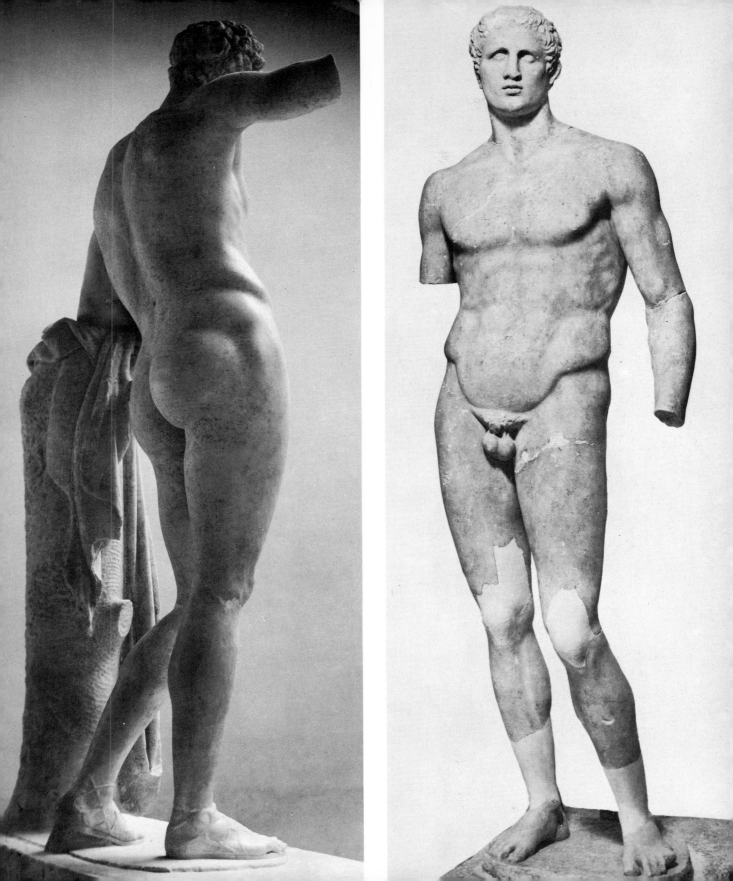

7 *Young boy c.* 350 B.C.
Athens, National Museum

8 SCOPAS?
Meleager original *c.* 340–330 B.C.,
Roman copy *c.* A.D. 100
Cambridge, Mass., Fogg Art
Museum, Harvard University

9 LEOCHARES?
  Apollo of Belvedere original 320 B.C.,
  Roman copy
  Vatican, Musei e Gallerie Pontificie,
  Cortile del Belvedere

0 *Funerary stele* 330 B.C.
  Athens, National Museum

161 *Mausolos, Satrap of Caria c.* 350 B.C.
London, British Museum

162 *Tissaphernes, Satrap of western Asia
Minor* 412 B.C.
London, British Museum

163 *Mausolos,* detail of 161 (*right*)

4 PRAXITELES?
Head of Hermes, detail of 155

165 *Head of Agias*,
detail of 156

166 SCOPAS?
Head of Meleager, detail of 158

SILANION
Plato original 360 B.C., Roman copy
Private collection

168 SILANION?
Head of a boxer, profile view of 169

169 SILANION?
Head of a boxer 330 B.C.
Athens, National Museum

LATE CLASSICAL GREEK

170 KEPHISODOTOS
    '*Peace and Wealth*' original 370 B.C.
    Roman copy
    Munich, Antikensammlung

171 *Athena c.* 350 B.C.
    Piraeus, Museum

172 *Demeter c.* 350 B.C.
   Izmir, Archaeological Museum

173 *Demeter c.* 330 B.C.
   London, British Museum

174 *Victory tying her sandal* 410–405 B.
Athens, Acropolis Museum

175 PRAXITELES
Aphrodite original *c.* 370 B.C.,
Roman copy
Vatican

176 *Hera Eileithyia?* 370 B.C.
Paestum, Museum

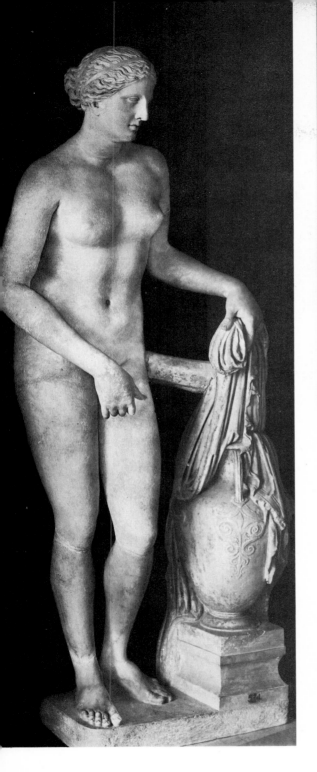

177 *Head of Aphrodite c.* 340 B.C.
Boston, Museum of Fine Arts

178 *Muse? Artemis? c.* 350 B.
Piraeus, Museum

9 *Ariadne* c. 340 B.C.
Athens, National Museum

180 *Head of goddess* c. 320–300 B.C.
Taranto, Museo Archeologico

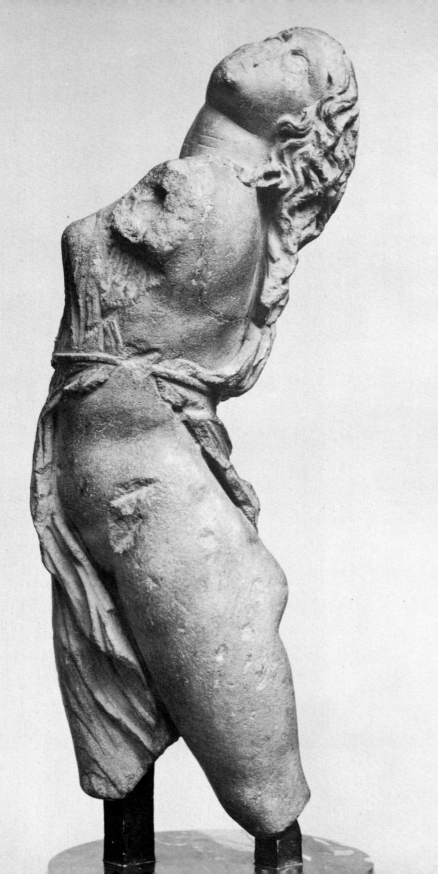

188 *Victory driving chariot* 375–350 B.C.
Boston, Museum of Fine Arts

RADIATION TO PERIPHERY: ETRUSCAN

189 *Man and woman c.* 675–650 B.C.
Florence, Museo Archeologico

190 *Sphinx c.* 650 B.C.
Rome, Museo Preistorico

191 *Nude goddess* 675–650 B.C.
Florence, Museo Archeologico

192 *Nude goddess,* view from
the back of 191

Head from burial urn c. 650–625 B.C.
Siena, Museo Archeologico Senese

Goddess on lid of cinerary urn
650 B.C.
Chiusi, Museo Civico

Caryatids c. 600 B.C.
Rome, Museo di Villa Giulia

196 *Peleus and Thetis* 540 B.C.
  Munich, Staatliche Antikensammlung

197 VULCA?
  Apollo 500 B.C.
  Rome, Museo di Villa Giulia

8 *Athena, Tinia and giants* 480–470 B.C. 199 *Winged horses* 350–300 B.C.
  Rome, Museo di Villa Giulia   Tarquinia, Museo Nazionale

Tinia? (*Etruscan Zeus*) 450 B.C.
Kansas City, Missouri, William
Rockhill Nelson Collection

201 *Chimaera c.* 350 B.C.
Florence, Museo Archeologico

Fleeing girl 350 B.C.
Florence, Museo Archeologico

Demons and ambush scene
4th cent. B.C.
Vulci, Sarcophagus

Portrait of the dead, a battle scene
c. 150 B.C.
Worcester, Massachusetts, Art Museum

207 *Charun*, left end of urn in Worcester, 206

210 *Velthur Partunus* 250–200 B.C.
Tarquinia, Museo Nazionale

211 *Unknown man* 120–100 B.C.
Copenhagen, Ny Carlsberg Glyptotek

2 *Head of a boy* 150–100 B.C.
   Florence, Museo Archeologico

3 *Head of a priest?* *c.* 250 B.C.
   London, British Museum

214 *Head of Aule Metelis (see 28*
100–80 B.C.
Florence, Museo Archeologico

215 *Head of a man* 80–50 B.C.
Rome, Museo di Villa Giulia

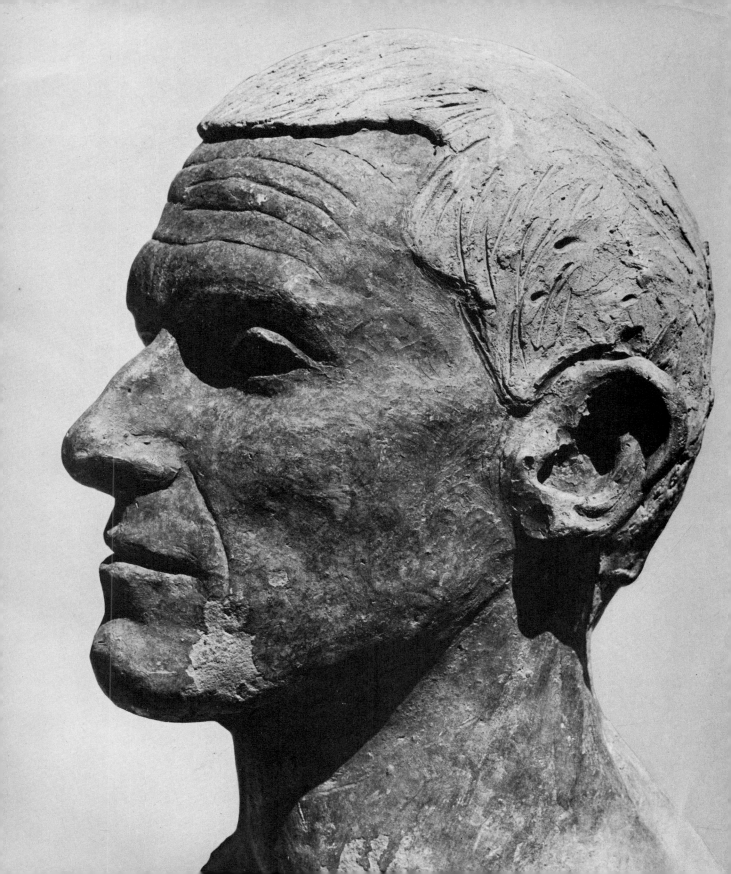

216 Iberian
The Lady of Elche 4th–3rd cent. B.C.
Madrid, Prado

217 Greek, found in Near E
'Penelope' c. 400 B.C.
Teheran, Museum

218 Scythian
Scythian extracting arrow c. 380 F
Leningrad, Hermitage

219 Scythian
Animal contest – battle scene c. 400 F
New York, Metropolitan Muse·
(*below*)

HELLENISTIC SCULPTURE

220 *Alexander with lion helmet,* detai
battle scene (*see also* 222)

221 *Head of Alexander the Great*
c. 160 B.C.
Istanbul, Archaeological Museum

222 *Alexander's hunt and battle*
c. 320 B.C. (*see* VI)
Istanbul, Archaeological Museum

3 *Head of Alexander the Great* 3rd cent. B.C.
Alexandria, Greco-Roman Museum

4 *Alexander* original 320–310 B.C., Hellenistic copy
Paris, Louvre

225 *Aristotle* original *c.* 330 B.C.,
Roman copy
Vienna, Kunsthistorisches
Museum

226 *Head of Odysseus*, detail of 2

HELLENISTIC

230 PHANIS?
Sacrificing girl original *c.* 270–250 B.C
Roman copy
Rome, Museo Nazionale delle Ter

231 *Sacrificing girl*, detail of 230

Boy jockey, detail of 232

Boy jockey 230–200 B.C.
Athens, National Museum

235 *Nike*, detail of 234

236 *Athena fighting giants c.* 180–160 B.C.
Berlin, Staatliche Museen

7 Zeus fighting giants c. 180–160 B.C.
Berlin, Staatliche Museen

238 HAGESANDROS, ATHANADOROS, POLYDO
Odysseus' helmsman falling 175–150 B.C.
Sperlonga, Museum

HAGESANDROS, ATHANADOROS, POLYDOROS
Odysseus and Palladion 175–150 B.C.
Sperlonga, Museum

240 HAGESANDROS, ATHANADOROS,
POLYDOROS
Head of helmsman, detail of 238

241 *Dying giant* original 200–150 B.C.?,
Roman copy
Naples, Museo Nazionale

242 HAGESANDROS, ATHANADOROS,
POLYDOROS
Laocoön c. 150 B.C.
Vatican, Museums

243 *Heracles fighting centaur* origi[n]
150–100 B.C., Roman copy
Vienna, Kunsthistorisches Museu[m]

244 *Sleeping satyr c.* 200 B.C.
Munich, Antikensammlung

15 APOLLONIOS, SON OF NESTOR
  Torso c. 100 B.C.
  Vatican, Atrio del Torso

16 *Boxer c.* 100–70 B.C.
  Rome, Museo Nazionale delle
  Terme

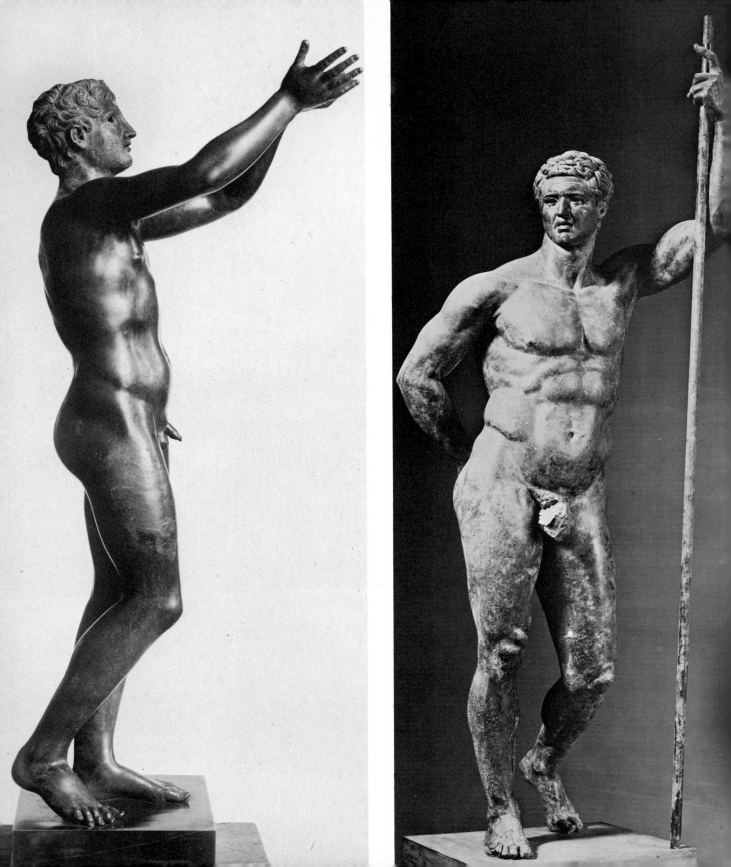

7 *Praying boy c.* 300 B.C.
  Berlin, Staatliche Museen

248 *Hellenistic prince c.* 150 B.C.
  Rome, Museo Nazionale
  delle Terme

249 *'Borghese' warrior* original *c.* 100 B.C.,
  Roman copy
  Paris, Louvre

250 *Emaciated man* original 300–250 B.
Roman copy
Washington, D.C., Dumbart
Oaks Collection

251 *Menander and Archilochos c.* A.D.
Paris, Louvre

252 *Comic actor and mime*
4th–3rd cent. B.C.
Taranto, Museum

253 *Sleeping Eros c. 250–200 B.C.*
New York, Metropolitan Museum

4 '*Capitoline Venus*' original 300–250 B.C.,
Roman copy
Rome, Museo Capitolino

255 *Aphrodite, Pan, Eros* original
100–80 B.C., Roman copy
Athens, National Museum

256 (AGAS?)ANDROS
Aphrodite c. 150–120 B.C.
Paris, Louvre

257 *Venus de' Medici* original
150–100 B.C., Roman copy
Florence, Galleria degli Uffizi

Head of Venus de' Medici, detail of 257

Female head c. 160–150 B.C. ?
Berlin, Staatliche Museen

260 *Artemis and satyrs at altar* 120 B.C.
Delos, Temple of Good Fortune

261 *Cleopatra and Dioscourides* 137 B.C.
Delos, House of Cleopatra and
Dioscourides

262 *Cleopatra VII* 51–30 B.C., coin (
Alexandria
Boston, Museum of Fine Arts

263 *Euthydemos of Bactria*? original
c. 200 B.C., Roman copy
Rome, Villa Albani

264 *Juba II?* 20 B.C.
Rabat, Musée des Antiquités Pré-
Islamiques

265 *Homer* original *c.* 150 B.C.
Late Hellenistic copy
Boston, Museum of Fine Arts

266 *Gaul killing himself* original
220 B.C., Roman copy
Rome, Museo Nazionale de
Terme

267 APOLLONIOS AND TAURISKOS
Punishment of Dirke original
c. 150 B.C., Roman copy
Naples, Museo Nazionale

268 *Three Graces* original
c. 150–100 B.C., Roman copy
Siena, Cathedral Museum

269 ARCHELAOS OF PRIENE
Apotheosis of Homer c. 125 B.C.
London, British Museum

270 *Building Auge's ark c.* 160 B.C.
Berlin, Staatliche Museen

271 *Lioness and cubs in a cave* 20 B.C.?
Vienna, Kunsthistorisches Museum

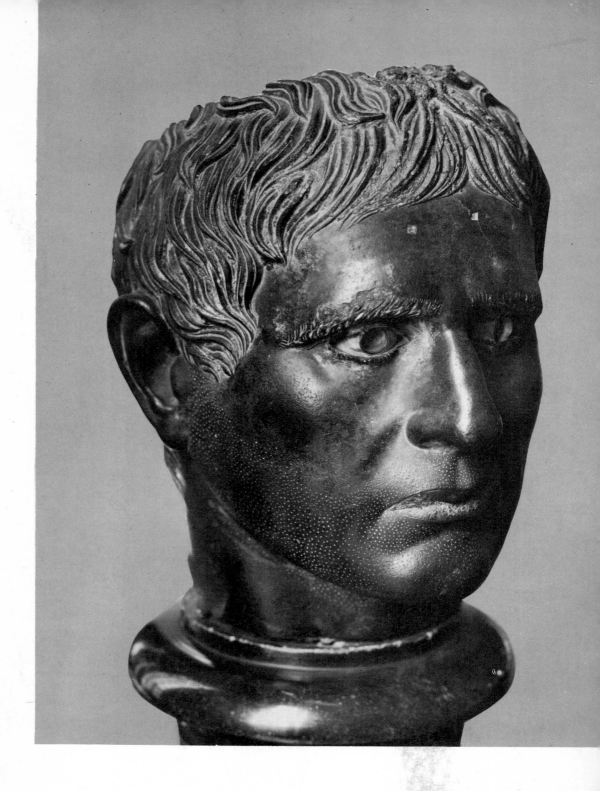

2 Samnite
Head of a man 150–100 B.C.
Paris, Bibliothèque Nationale

3 Celtic
God with stag's feet c. 100 B.C.
Saint-Germain-en-Laye, Musée des
Antiquités Nationales

274 ANTIOCHOS, SON OF DRYAS
Mousa, wife of Phraates IV 37–32 B.C.?
Teheran, Archaeological Museum

275 CHEIRISOPHOS
Priam and Achilles c. 20 B.C.
Copenhagen, National Museum

Irano–Hellenistic
Mithridates Kallinikos and Heracles c. 50 B.C.
Burial mound of Arsameia Commagene

277 Parthian
Satrap before 139 B.C.?
Teheran, Archaeological Museum

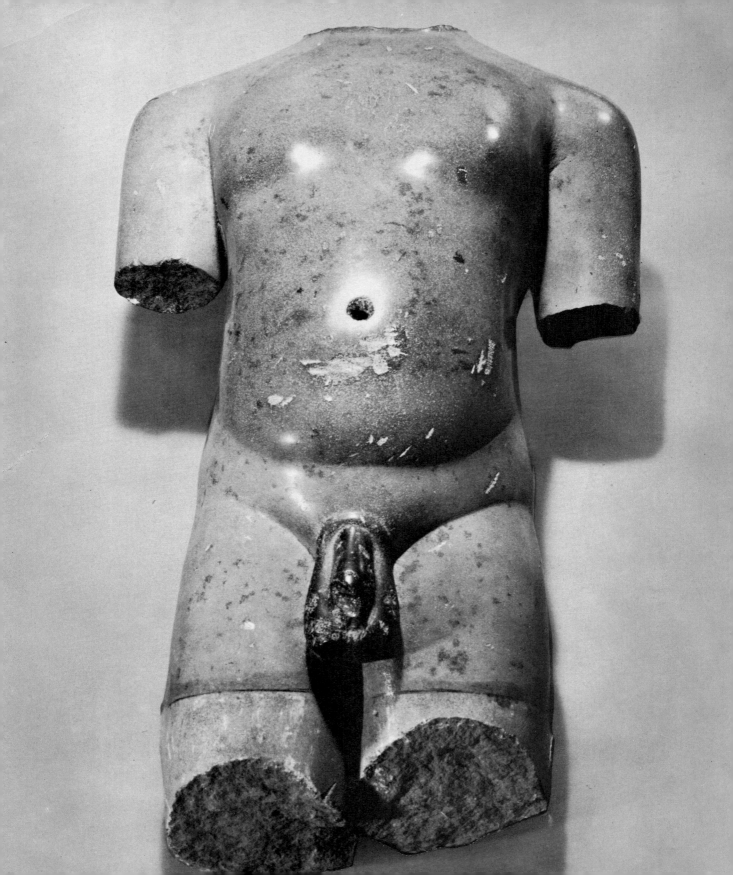

8 Indian
Torso of nude c. 200 B.C.
Patna, Museum

279 South Arabian
Eros riding on lioness c. 75–50 B.C.
Washington, D.C., Smithsonian Institution and
American Foundation for the Study of Man

ROMAN IMPERIAL SCULPTURE

2 *Republican general c.* 80–60 B.C.
Rome, Museo Nazionale
delle Terme

283 MENELAOS
Orestes and Electra c. A.D. 10?
Rome, Museo Nazionale
delle Terme

284 *Roman couple* 50–40 B.C.
Rome, Museo Nuovo Capitolino

288 *Head of Augustus*, detail of 287

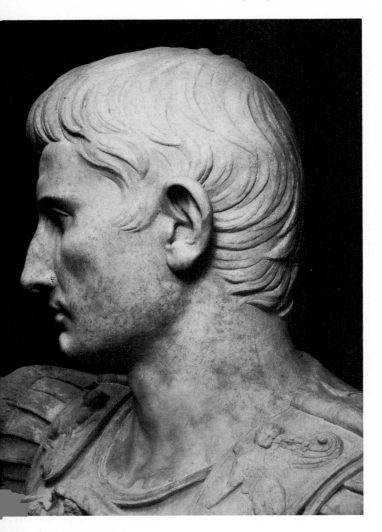

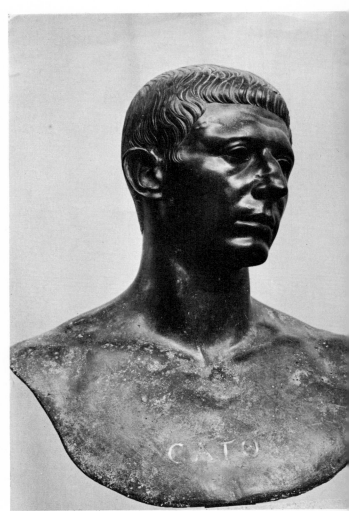

289 *Cato Uticensis* original 50 B.C.,
copy *c.* A.D. 100?
Rabat, Musée des Antiquités Pr
Islamiques

291 *Altar of Augustan Peace* 13–9 B.C.
Rome, Via di Ripetta

292 *Triumphal procession c.* 20 B.C.
Rome, Palazzo Conservatori

293 *Family of Augustus* south side of

294 *The Menorah of the Temple Jerusalem* A.D. 81, detail of 295

295 *Triumphal Procession, Spoils Jerusalem* A.D. 81
Rome, Arch of Titus, south panel of passage

96 *Triumph of Titus* A.D. 81
Rome, Arch of Titus, northern
panel of passage

7 *Column of Trajan* A.D. 113
   Rome, Forum of Trajan

8 *Column of Trajan*,
   four lowest windings

299 *Exedra of 'Canopus'*
Tivoli, Villa of Hadrian

300 *Antinous c.* A.D. 130
Naples, Museo Nazionale

301 *Mithras* A.D. 180–200
London, Guildhall Museum

302 *Caius Volcacius Myropnous*
c. A.D. 150
Ostia, Museo Ostiense

303 *Sabina as Venus c.* A.D. 130
Ostia, Museo Ostiense

4 *Diana of Ephesus*, detail of 305

305 *Diana of Ephesus* A.D. 130–40
Selçuk, Museum

306 *Cavalry parade, Column of Antoninus*
A.D. 161–5
Vatican, Museums, Giardino della Pi

7 *Column of Marcus Aurelius* A.D. 180–93
Rome, Piazza Colonna

8 *Marcus Aurelius c.* A.D. 165
Rome, Piazza di Campidoglio

9 *Marcus Aurelius*, detail of 308

310 *Julia sacrifices to Severus and Roma*
A.D. 203
Tripoli, Museum

311 *Julia Domna as Ceres* after A.D. 217
Ostia, Museo Ostiense

2 *Achilles–Penthesilea sarcophagus* A.D. 250
Vatican, Museums, Cortile del Belvedere

313 *Small arch of Galerius c.* A.D. 300
Thessaloniki, Museum

314 *Persian campaign of Galerius* after
A.D. 298
Thessaloniki, Arch of Galerius

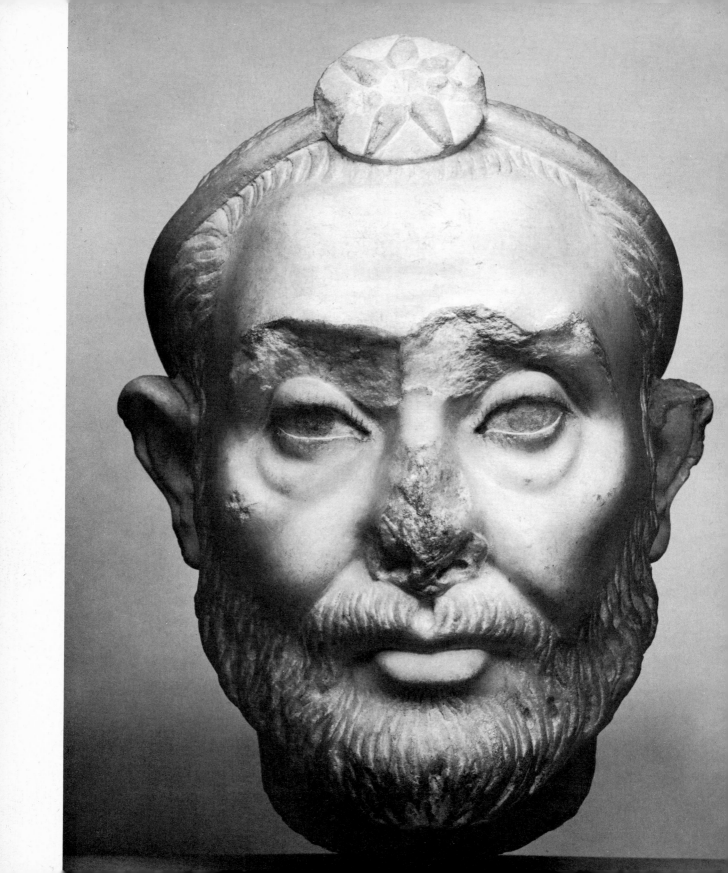

5 *Priest of Serapis c.* A.D. 230–50
Berlin, Staatliche Museen

316 *Flavius Damianus c.* A.D. 180
Selçuk, Museum

317 *Man in toga c.* A.D. 380–400
Ostia, Museo Ostiense

ROMAN IMPERIAL

318 *Constantine c.* A.D. 330
Rome, Palazzo Conservatori

9 *Emperor Gallienus* A.D. 260–8
Copenhagen, Ny Carlsberg
Glyptotek

320 *Claudia Antonia Sabina* A.D. 215
Istanbul, Archaeological Museum

321 *Portrait of a lady* A.D. 240–50
Alexandria, Greco-Roman
Museum

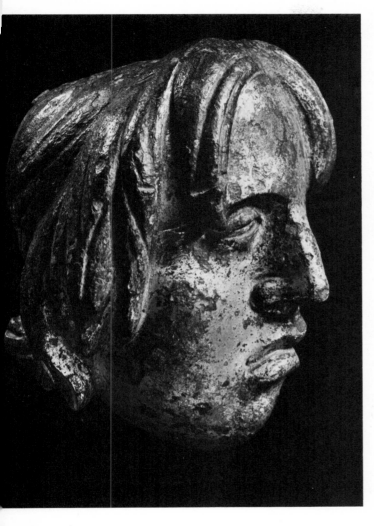

Roman Gaul
Head of a Helvetian 2nd cent. A.D.
Avenches, Musée romain

323 Roman Britain
Head-pot depicting woman early 3rd cent. A.D.
York, Yorkshire Museum

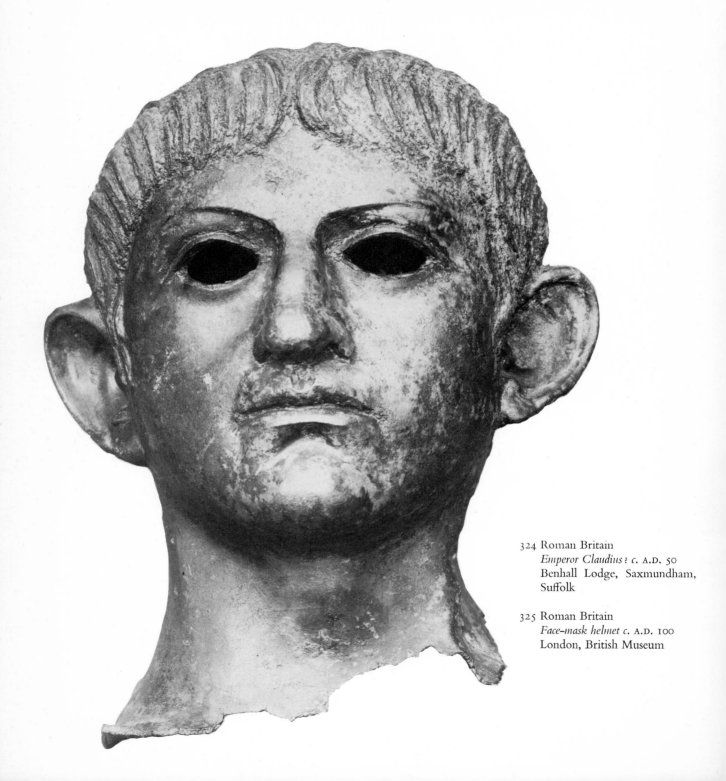

324 Roman Britain
Emperor Claudius? c. A.D. 50
Benhall Lodge, Saxmundham,
Suffolk

325 Roman Britain
Face-mask helmet c. A.D. 100
London, British Museum

326 Roman Gaul
Lion attacking gladiator 1st cent. A.D.
Chalon-sur-Saône, Musée Denon

327 Roman Gaul
Altar to the Aufanian Mothers A.D. 164
Bonn, Rheinisches Landesmuseum

328 Palmyrene
Funerary portraits c. A.D. 175–200
Damascus, Museum

39 Gandharan
Standing Buddha c. A.D. 100
Formerly in the Guides' Mess,
Hoti-Mardan, near Peshawar

40 Gandharan
Buddha's great renunciation
2nd cent. A.D.
Calcutta, Indian Museum

LATE ROMAN
AND EARLY
CHRISTIAN
SCULPTURE

41 *Good Shepherd c.* A.D. 250
Varennes, France, Church of
Brignoles

332 Coptic
   Daniel in the lions' den c. A.D. 500
   Washington, D.C., Dumbarton
   Oaks Collection

LATE ROMAN
AND EARLY CHRISTIAN

333 Coptic
   Dancing nereids 5th cent. A.D.
   Trieste, Civico Museo di Storia ed A

Arch of Constantine A.D. 312–15
Rome

335 *People listening to Constantine*,
detail of 334 (left side, central frieze)

336 *Sarcophagus of Constantia c.* A.D. 330
Vatican, Museums, Sala della Croce Gre

Sarcophagus A.D. 385–90
Milan, S. Ambrogio

338 *Sarcophagus of Adelfia c.* A.D. 340
Syracuse, Museo Archeologico

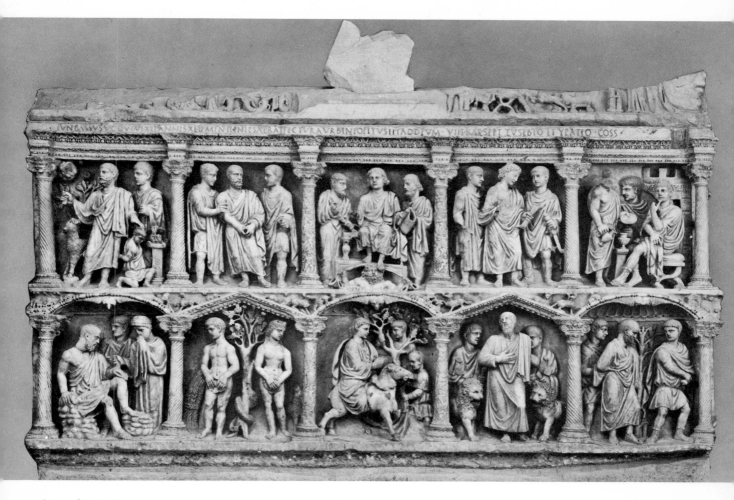

9 Sarcophagus of Junius Bassus A.D. 359
Vatican, Crypt of St Peter

340 *Adam and Eve*, detail of 339

1 *Death of Judas: Crucifixion* c. A.D. 420
   London, British Museum

344 *Triumphant emperor* 6th cent. A.D.
Barletta, in front of S. Sepolcro

345 *Constantius II* A.D. 324–61
Rome, Palazzo Conservatori, Sa
dei Bronzi

6 *Evangelist* 5th cent. A.D.
Istanbul, Archaeological Museum

347 *Adoration of Magi* c. A.D. 420
Ravenna, S. Vitale

LATE ROMAN
AND EARLY CHRISTIAN

348 *Heracles and Nemean lion* 6th cent. A.D
Paris, Cabinet des Médailles

NOTES ON THE COLOUR PLATES

Measurements are given in the order height, width, depth unless otherwise indicated.

NOTE ON BIBLIOGRAPHICAL REFERENCES Where the author's last name only is cited, see *Bibliography* for full details. Abbreviated title refers to second or subsequent work by an author (see also *Bibliography*). With single references, details are cited in full in Notes only. Abbreviations of periodicals follow the list published by the *American Journal of Archaeology* 62, 1958.

I
II
III
IV
V
VI
VII
VIII

MYCENAEAN GREECE

I *Sphinx?* c. 1300 B.C.? plaster relief 0·168 m.
Mycenae
Athens, National Museum
Strange in its bright coloured features and tattoo, wearing a fillet or cap, eyes floating on bony face, mouth grim, this rare example of life-size sculpture shows potential tectonic strength not fully organized. Some think the face belonged to a goddess.
Marinatos pl. 43. E. Vermeule pl. 40.

ARCHAIC GREECE

II *Dioscuri, Linus, Orpheus and the Argo* c. 560 B.C. painted limestone 0·53 m.
Metope, Treasury of Sicyon, Delphi
Delphi, Museum
Flanked by boldly frontal Dioscuri, the boat of the Argonauts lands to music by Linus and Orpheus (inscribed 'Orphas'). Another Argonaut (now lost) held spear. Vying with epic, the sculptors tell many stories in a circumstantial, miniaturistic style in high relief, gay with polychromy.
Picard 1, fig. 148. P. de la Coste-Messelière, *Delphes*, 1943, fig. 42.

ARCHAIC GREECE

III *An Athenian girl* c. 510 B.C. painted marble H. 0·555 m.
Acropolis, Athens
Athens, Acropolis Museum
A lady is known by the way she picks up her skirt, taught the poetess, Sappho. Delicate, fashionable, the girl presents an ornate front; the back is much simpler. Archaic mannerism triumphs in dazzling displays of folds and hair: a poem to the courtly ideal.
Payne pl. 49: 3–4.

ETRUSCAN

IV VULCA? *Goddess and child* c. 500 B.C. painted terracotta 1·43 m.
From roof-beam, Temple of Portonaccio, Veii
Rome, Museo di Villa Giulia
Long legs, bony hands, small head, but the folds, which lead their own life, are as on the statue of Apollo (197). Probably part of the same scene, she is fleeing from the fight – 'a frenzied *sauve qui peut* look about her eyes, but she smiles too' (Richardson).
Richardson, 101. M. Pallottino, *La scuola di Vulca*, 1945, pls. 7–9.

EARLY CLASSICAL GREECE

V *Three sileni* c. 480 B.C. painted terracotta tallest 0·113 m.
Megara
New York, Norbert Schimmel Collection
As a satyrplay is to Anacreon's dainty poems, so are these inebriate ithyphalics to the Archaic *korai*. Greek terracottas at their best are fine sculptures, sometimes freer and more adventurous than monumental statues. No Early Classical group is more expressive or more humorous.
H. Hoffmann, *Norbert Schimmel Coll.* 1964, no. 20; *Antike Kunst*, 1964.

HELLENISTIC

VI *Battle scene* c. 320 B.C. painted marble relief 0·45 m.
Crypt of Kings of Sidon, Sarcophagus of Abdalonymos
Istanbul, Archaeological Museum
When discovered in 1887 the sarcophagus glowed in colours much faded since. Here, in an artist's attempt to reproduce the original polychromy, we see the advance of Late Classical Greek painting towards a highly diversified palette which contributed to the lifelikeness of marble sculpture, permitting a refined rendering of emotions. One of Alexander's generals battles down a Persian while infantry fights in the background.
For other views, *see* 220, 222. Reuterswärd, 60.

ROMAN

VII *Statue of Mars* c. A.D. 70 Pompeian painting pedestal and figure c. 2.10 m.
Pompeii, Casa di Venere
Helen (32) would have to jump to embrace this statue. A wonderful testimonial both for original effect of a coloured statue of Classical (c. 400 B.C. *Ares Borghese*) type and Roman manner of displaying statues raised up as decorative accents against the green of landscaped gardens.
Reuterswärd, frontispiece.

ROMAN

VIII HADRIAN *Aphrodite of Knidos in the Round Temple* Roman copy A.D. 121–38
Tivoli, Villa of Hadrian
Picturesque Pompeian fantasy is translated into romantic reality by the Emperor turned architect. Against the soft beauty of Roman Campagna, temple and statue invoke Classical Greece as the major component in Hadrian's vision of a cosmopolitan, pantheistic world.
K. Schefold, *Antike Kunst*, 1964, 56. *See* 176.

NOTES ON THE MONOCHROME ILLUSTRATIONS

Measurements are given in the order height, width, depth unless otherwise indicated. Asterisk ★ indicates alternative view of main picture.

1

2

3

4

5

6

7★

THE FORERUNNERS

NEOLITHIC ANATOLIA

1 *Goddess and young god c.* 5400 B.C. burnished terracotta L. 0·12 m
House Q5, Level VI, Hacilar, Southwest Asia Minor
Ankara, Hittite Museum
A school of great sculptors flourished in the Neolithic village oɪ Hacilar. This complex, bold group is a symbol of the miracle of generation. It shows the earth goddess and her young lover, who fertilizes her, dies, and is revived. Her body is stirring, awakening to life.
Zervos, *Naissance* 2 fig. 614.

EARLY BRONZE AGE GREECE

2 *Phallic man c.* 2500 B.C. terracotta 0·49 m.
Thessaly
Athens, National Museum
The seated posture means first authority, dignity, then repose. The volumes are simple and powerful, the expression aggressive. What links this work with Classical art is monumentality – this is no longer a talisman to be handled, but a small statue to be worshipped.
Zervos, *Naissance* 2 figs. 501–2.

CYCLADIC ISLANDS

3 *Female idol c.* 2400 B.C. marble 0·159 m.
Boston, Museum of Fine Arts
Cycladic sculptors anticipated two basic traits of the Classical ideal – belief in geometric structure and exploitation of the beauty of marble. Under their vigorous abstractionism the opulent 'Great Woman' who dominated the Stone Age is reduced to an icon, a protecting symbol laid down next to the dead.
E. Vermeule, 52. Zervos, *Cyclades* fig. 161.

4 *Harpist c.* 2000 B.C. marble 0·225 m.
Grave on island of Keros, Greece
Athens, National Museum
Three right angles, three curving forms are combined in striking simplicity. The musician looks blind and inspired. Does he sing an incantation to the goddess who protects the dead? In Greek myth Orpheus descends to the nether world, enchants the rulers of the dead, and returns alive. Zervos, *Cyclades* pl. 333.

MINOAN CRETE

5 *Bull jumper* 16th century B.C. ivory L. 0·299 m.
Palace of Knossos, Crete
Heraklion, Archaeological Museum
'This carving reaches the most exquisite level of miniature sculpture attained in the ancient world.' (J. D. S. Pendlebury). In sacral athletics and art Minoans pioneered the idea of the male nude form, which Classical Greece revived; but their sculptors interpreted the virile body as streamlined motion, not as solid, structured reality.
J. D. S. Pendlebury, *Archaeology of Crete*, 1939, pl. 39:1.

6 *Praying woman* 16th century B.C. bronze 0·19 m.
The Troad?
Berlin, Staatliche Museen
I have seen a young Greek girl sweep into the dark church, genuflect, sweep out again, long skirts trailing. The artist has caught her Minoan ancestress unawares – the quick movement, the unselfconscious absorption. Rough, unfinished surface adds that suggestion of life emerging from matter, which Michelangelo and Rodin were to elaborate. Three snakes twist about her neck and head; she is a devotee of the great Snake Goddess worshipped throughout Minoan Crete.
Lamb pl. 7a.

7 *Worshipping youth c.* 1500 B.C. bronze 0·173 m.
New York, Walter C. Baker Collection
In Minoan bronze sculpture willowy athletes appear as worshippers. They have long legs, thin waists, and small heads only one-eighth of the height of the body. In profile a curve throws head and shoulders far back of the vertical axis as the youth tenses to stand 'at attention'. The eye is floating, vague. The best examples attain a disciplined dignity of posture which foreshadows Archaic Greek *kouroi*.
Fogg, 1954, pl. 35.

8 *Boxing scene c.* 1500 B.C. steatite 0·465 m. (without handle)
Hagia Triada
Heraklion, Archaeological Museum
Minoan Crete bequeathed to Classical Greece athletic sports as an offering pleasing to gods. A pouring vessel from a Royal Lodge depicts the events: broad jump (?), bull jumping, boxing, wrestling (?).

8   9   10   1   12   13★   14   15

The boxers wore heavy 'crash-helmets', leather thongs for gloves, tight trunks, gaiters. Within the four superposed zones the figures move in restless rhythms. They speak through their postures. Here the victor, of sprawling gait, flexes his bulging muscles.
Marinatos figs. 106 ff. Platon pl. 9.

9 *Sacred mountain* 1500 B.C. grey stone
Royal Hall, Palace of Kato Zakro
Heraklion, Archaeological Museum
Terraces of neat masonry support sacred horns, altars and a shrine on a scaly mountain. Reclining on the roof, two pairs of engaging mountain goats flank the sacred stone. Hawks fly over the colonnaded wings. Animals and their invisible protectress rule this mountain; man is absent.
Society of Hellenic Studies, *Archaeological reports for 1963-4* fig. 39.

MYCENAEAN GREECE
10 *Lion gate* 13th century B.C. limestone relief 3·02 m.
Mycenae
The first of all heraldic castle gates of Europe thrills the visitor with its rude majesty; this threshold Agamemnon crossed going to his death. The mighty triangle of lions is enlarged from Minoan gems, yet these fierce guardians are as monumentally defiant as the legendary rulers of Mycenae.
Marinatos fig. 141.

MINOAN CRETE?
11 *Smiling youth* 14th century B.C. lead 0·12 m.
A grave at Kampos, Laconia
Athens, National Museum
The 'archaic smile' of Greek *kouroi* seems static compared to the fluid grin which plays over this face. The boy seems pleased with himself: 'Look what a big fish I have caught.' The natural expression of optimism is a striking accomplishment in a work of the Bronze Age.
Marinatos pl. 224.

MYCENAEAN GREECE
12 *Head of a king* 16th century B.C. amethyst 0·01 m.
Grave Gamma, Circle 'B', Mycenae
Athens, National Museum

'There were strong men before Agamemnon.' One of them is shown in this gem, with wild hair and beard, heavy eyebrows, stub nose, a grim grin. Accustomed to show royalty as small-headed and clean-shaven, the Minoan artist had an obvious struggle, but caught something of his patron's aggressive energy.
E. Vermeule pl. 11C. Marinatos fig. 212.

CYPRUS
13 *God with horned cap* 12th century B.C. bronze 0·55 m.
Ashlar Building, Room X, Enkomi
Nicosia, Cyprus Museum
The full-cast, ponderous statue of the horned god from 'Coppertown' (Alasiya) on the 'Copper Island' (Cyprus) demands respect and attention. Aegean tension and Oriental stolidity, fluid outlines and voluminous flesh, are convincingly fused. Worshipped amidst sacrificed oxen, the image was hidden in a pit when the final catastrophe struck.
H. Catling, *Cypriot bronzework*, 1964, pl. 46.

CYCLADIC-MINOAN (KEOS)
14 *Female figure* 1500 B.C. terracotta 0·988 m.
Keos, Temple at Ayia Irini
The island shrine at St Irene on Keos has produced remnants of twenty terracotta statues. Their skirts flattened, naked white breasts jumping forward, hesitant smiles – are they goddesses 'benignly at home' or priestesses dancing in ecstasy? They have the awkwardness of enlarged miniatures and a rustic friendliness.
Caskey, *Hesperia*, 1964, pl. 61. E. Vermeule pl. 40.

MYCENAEAN GREECE
15 *Head of Poseidon*? 12th century B.C. terracotta 0·12 m.
Lower Town, House G, Asine
Nauplion, Museum
The sea beats against the grey rock of Asine. Is this Poseidon, lord of the sea, whom the Swedish archaeologists discovered in a small shrine? Because the head was painted white some have thought it a goddess. The angular expressiveness befits the Viking-like seafaring age that preceded the dawn of historic Greece.
O. Frödin, A. Persson, *Asine*, 1922–30, fig. 211. E. Vermeule, 285.

18

20

16   17   19   21   22   23   24★

GEOMETRIC SCULPTURE
OF GREECE

16 *Stag* 'Protogeometric' 11th century B.C. terracotta 0·26 m.
Grave 39, Kerameikos Cemetery, Athens
Athens, Kerameikos Museum
This strange animal illustrates the very beginning of Greek Geometric style. From the back the deer looks barrel-shaped, bow-legged; in profile vertical legs and proud neck make architecture out of sculpture. The painted geometric pattern, a sliding blanket, loosely covers the forms. The eye blobs in the black face are fixed in a snooty glance.
Karo pl. 8. Matz fig. 23.

17 *Horse* 8th century B.C. bronze 0·176 m.
New York, Metropolitan Museum
'Horse-breeding' is Homer's word for rich grazing land; horses are the hall-mark of Greek aristocracy. Favourite theme of the new geometry in art, favourite offering to gods, the best of these small bronzes are among the noblest abstractions achieved in any sculpture.
Himmelmann-Wildschütz fig. 61.

18 *Deer and fawn* 750–700 B.C. bronze 0·072 m.
Thebes
Boston, Museum of Fine Arts
Mother's patient air, the eager nuzzling of the fawn on its thin, sliding legs, the bird alighting on the crupper of the deer, combine in a delicate abstraction to make us smile at the gentle humour of this Geometric Klee.
Boston, 1963, fig. 26.

19 *Dancing women* 8th century B.C. bronze *c.* 0·075 m.
Olympia
Athens, National Museum
Athletic games and dances were offerings to the gods. This group was probably given for victory in a dancing contest in honour of Hera. Unity is emphasized as seven interlaced nudes stamp heavily in a circle; a remarkable experiment in group formation.
Charbonneaux pl. 5:3.

20 *Warrior* 8th century B.C. bronze 0·186 m.
New York, Metropolitan Museum
Near Eastern storm gods whose images were exported to Greece were models for this type, used in sanctuaries at Dodona and Olympia to represent Zeus as god of battle. Once the figure held spear and shield.
Richter, *Kouroi* figs. 3–5.

21 *Charioteer* 8th century B.C. bronze 0·145 m.
Olympia
Olympia, Museum
Races of battle chariots at the mound of legendary hero Pelops preceded the official founding of the Olympic Games (776 B.C.). Knees bent against jolts, the stocky warrior stares ahead. These bronzes are put together like toys, but their makers started the theme of the grandiose *Charioteer* of Delphi (99).
Himmelmann-Wildschütz fig. 39. Kunze, IV, pl. 35.

22 *Helmet-maker* 680–650 B.C. bronze 0·055 m.
New York, Metropolitan Museum
The poet Hesiod (seventh century B.C.) first praised industrious work. This helmet-maker may be divine, like Hephaistos who made armour for Achilles, but he is a craftsman at work, a '*genre* group', nonetheless. The sinuous composition bends angular forms to the flow of motion.
Richter, *Handbook* fig. 251. Himmelmann-Wildschütz figs. 49 ff.

23 *Running man* early 7th century B.C. bronze 0·105 m.
Paris, George Ortiz Collection
Rhythmic running is much emphasized in this remarkably free bronze. Triangular head and swelling buttocks are the only vestiges of Geometric bondage. The foot race was the earliest recorded Olympic event (776 B.C.), and this may be a present to the god by one of the winners.
Fogg, 1954, pl. 58.

GREEK ARCHAIC SCULPTURE

24 *Goddess or votary c.* 750–725 B.C. ivory 0·24 m.
Dipylon, Athens
Athens, National Museum

25

26

27

28*

29

30*

31

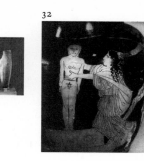
32

Five nudes of ivory from a grave which contained purely Geometric vases are closely modelled on Phoenician ivories of the love goddess Astarte. Yet structure and proportions are unmistakably Geometric Greek – the first appearance of Aphrodite in Greek sculpture.
Matz figs. 28a-b. Barnett 45, 51, 103 ff., on Near Eastern models.

5 *Priestess* 570–550 B.C. ivory 0·107 m.
Under image base of Archaic Temple of Artemis, Ephesus
Istanbul, Archaeological Museum
Clad in gorgeous robes such as Sappho's pupils loved, the girl holds sacrificial bowl and jug; balanced on her head was a pole surmounted by the sacred hawk of Artemis. 'One might feel oneself reminded of her by Foolish Virgins in a French cathedral of the early thirteenth century.' (P. Jacobsthal).
P. Jacobsthal, *JHS*, 1951, 92, pl. 34. Akurgal fig. 172.

6 *Apollo c.* 650 B.C. bronze 0·80 m.
With Artemis and Leto, platform right rear corner, Temple of Dreros, Crete
Heraklion, Archaeological Museum
Hidden in a saddle between grey mountains, the Shrine of Dreros is no larger than a hut, but of highest interest for the formative period of the Greek temple. The statues were hammered in sheets of bronze over wooden cores. *Apollo*, the tallest, is much repaired. The sculptor works towards largeness of form but has not as yet attained disciplined monumentality.
Richter, *Kouroi* fig. 12. Demargne figs. 453–5.

7 *Two goddesses?* 650–625 B.C. ivory 0·137 m.
New York, Metropolitan Museum; perhaps from a chest
In this open-work relief the change from constructivist, additive geometry to monumental coherence of the 'Daedalic' style is strikingly evident. A dramatic moment, and an unusual subject; the woman on the left is loosening her belt; her left breast is already exposed. The one on the right reveals the splendour of her limbs as her richly ornamented garment falls to her feet. The story is enigmatic – Aphrodite and Peitho, goddess of persuasion, or mythical virgins from the Far North who served Artemis on Delos?
Richter, *AJA*, 49, 261. Matz pl. 289. Boardman fig. 33.

28 *Kneeling youth c.* 625 B.C. ivory 0·145 m.
Precinct of Hera, Samos
Athens, National Museum
This joyful, slender, large-headed boy served as support of some utilitarian object. Eyes, brows, pubes, ear-rings were inlaid in paste. The masterly carving of ivory shows how quickly the Greeks learned; only the ornate pattern of belt and hair recalls the Oriental model.
Buschor fig. 245. Boardman fig. 32. Demargne fig. 496.

29 *Youth or warrior* 700–675 B.C. bronze 0·20 m.
Boeotia, perhaps from Sanctuary of Apollo in Thebes
Boston, Museum of Fine Arts
'Mantiklos dedicated me to the Far-Shooter of the Silver Bow, out of the tithe. Do Thou, Phoebus, give something nice in return.' The donor's prayer is engraved on the legs. The figure is strongly structured: pyramidal neck, columnar hair, elongated triangle of body, and bulging buttocks.
Richter, *Kouroi* fig. 9. Jeffery, 90, 402, pl. 7

30 *Male figure c.* 700 B.C. bronze 0·367 m.
Olympia
Olympia, Museum
Exaggeration of height and blind energy result in expressive form akin to some modern sculpture. The figure and its counterpart stood on the rim and held the handle of a large Geometric bronze cauldron.
Kunze, VII, pls. 62 f. Demargne fig. 405.

31 *Torso c.* 650 B.C. marble 0·85 m.
Delos
Delos, Museum
With the finest marble and best abrasive at their disposal, Cycladic sculptors on the islands of Paros and Naxos led Greece to monumental marble sculpture. The youth still wears the belt characteristic of Geometric nudes. This was perhaps the earliest life-size image of the famous *Kouros*-Apollo type.
Ritcher, *Kouroi* figs. 94–5.

32 *Early Archaic Apollo c.* 430 B.C. vase painting H. of vase 0·37 m.
Capua. Attic red-figure amphora
London, British Museum

35★

36

37

38★

39

33   34

To make statues accessible and real, Archaic artists used surprisingly low pedestals. If we take the Classical draughtsman literally, his *Apollo*, drawn after an Archaic statue, was about two-thirds life-size and stood on a two-stepped base about a foot high. The scene shows Menelaos seizing Helen.

Richter, *Kouroi* fig. 1. J. D. Beazley, *Attic red-figure vase painters*², 1010.

33 *Kriophoros c.* 600 B.C. marble 3·60 m.
Reused in Medieval citadel wall, Thasos
Thasos, Museum
Twice man's height, the huge slender youth clasps a pendent ram to his chest. Although unfinished, it is a beautiful early work, its clean long lines enhanced by pleasant yellow surface. He is either Hermes, protector of flocks, or an offering to Hermes.
Richter, *Kouroi* figs. 84–6, 106

34 (POLY?)MEDES OF ARGOS *Kleobis and Biton c.* 590 B.C. marble 2·18 m.
Northwest of Athenian Treasury, Delphi, probably both on an additional base
Delphi, Museum
Herodotus (1:31) says that these twins were taken by the gods as reward for piety. They are commemorated as optimistic young giants marching in unison. The squarish proportions and angular block structure distinguish workshops of mainland Greece. Inscribed on base of one statue: '. . . the sons carried. . . . medes of Argos made [them]', one of the earliest signatures in European sculpture.
Richter, *Kouroi* figs. 78–83, 91–2. Marcadé, 1, pl. 24, Jeffery, 155, pl. 26.

35 '*The Dipylon head*' *c.* 620 B.C. marble 0·44 m.
Dipylon Cemetery, Athens
Athens, National Museum
Crystalline majesty and mysterious grandeur combine in this earliest over life-size marble sculpture from Athens. There are traces of red colour on diadem. The statue was a youth; a hand certainly, a torso from the Athenian Agora possibly, belong.
Richter, *Kouroi* fig. 50. E. Harrison, *Hesperia*, 1955, 290.

36 *Goddess c.* 650 B.C. bronze 0·45 m.
Temple of Dreros, Crete
Heraklion, Archaeological Museum

Found with *Apollo* (26), *Artemis* displays a more compact form. A new loveliness emerges from charming responses of straight and curved lines, from wonderful individual touches – the hair combed straight down, the little breasts, and the engaging smile: 'What a good girl am I'.
Demargne fig. 452. Matz fig. 80a.

37 *Priestess? with distaff c.* 600 B.C. ivory 0·105 m.
Below Archaic Temple of Artemis, Ephesus
Istanbul, Archaeological Museum
Crowned and bejewelled, the woman holds a distaff; a spindle hangs on a thread from her right hand. With works such as this, Oriental masters active in Greece provided models for columnar form and exotic detail of Eastern Greek sculpture.
P. Jacobsthal, *JHS*, 71, 1951, pl. 25a–b. Akurgal fig. 197.

38 *Nikandre c.* 640 B.C. marble 1·75 m.
Sanctuary of Artemis, Delos
Athens, National Museum
'Nikandre dedicated me to the Farshooting Strong-Handed [goddess, Nikandre] daughter of Deinodikes of Naxos – outstanding above other women – of Deinomenes the sister; of Phraxos the wife.' The statue speaks the pride of aristocracy, pride in the monumental offering. The earliest Greek marble statue of a woman is a rectangular pillar softened by curves – from top of head through arms into curving back; countered through face and neck, hair, hanging breasts. The face is eroded; her hands are big and powerful.
Matz fig. 78. Papaspyridi, 19, no. 1.

39 *Protome of lion c.* 700 B.C. bronze 0·255 m.
Under Echo Hall, Olympia
Olympia, Museum
Cauldrons adorned with foreparts of lions were imported from metal-rich regions of the Near East into Greece. Their figurative decorations provided firmly established types and rich associations of religious symbolism for Greek artists seeking to express their own excited vision of the world of myth.
W. L. Brown, *The Etruscan Lion*, 1960, pl. 6 c 1.

40★

41

42

44

43

46

47

45

48

49

40 *Lion waterspout c.* 650 B.C. limestone L. 0·785 m.
Olympia
Olympia, Museum
The mask-like fierceness of the lion's face is still in Geometric taste; the neat stylization of mane, a favourite decorative device of Greek bronze-workers was taken over from the Near East. The work convincingly synthesizes these elements to portray a lean, murderous beast.
J. F. Crome, *Mnemosynon Th. Wiegand* pls. 7–10.

41 *Lion guarding grave c.* 600 B.C. painted limestone L. 1·22 m.
Near tomb of Menekrates, Korkyra
Korkyra, Museum
That a powerful creature should guard a grave was a belief developed in Egypt and known in Phoenicia. This work of ponderous strength by a sculptor from the famous school of Corinth stresses the lion's ferocious readiness in repose.
Rodenwaldt, *Korkyra 2*, 1939, fig. 154. Payne, *Necrocorinthia*, 1931, pl. 50:1.

42 *Lion c.* 525–500 B.C. marble L. *c.* 0·54 m.
Near Zopyrion Cave, Miletos
Berlin, Staatliche Museen
Early Archaic artists emphasized the demoniac fierceness of the lion. This Late Archaic lion is a masterly study in conscious abstraction; yet as the naturalistic hindpaws show, the sculptor had observed lions. The dejected, 'humanized' expression is perhaps intended to show grief over the dead, whose monument the lion guarded, rather than sorrow in captivity.
Blümel figs. 179–183. Richter, *Animals in Greek sculpture*, 1930, fig. 10.

43 *Lion*, view from back of 42

44 *Lions at Sacred Lake c.* 620 B.C. marble 1·28 m.
Delos, Sacred Road
Roaring in chorus, this phalanx of lions greeted the birth of their mistress, Artemis, on an island in the lake. Inspired by distant memories of Egyptian sacred roads and dim notions of lions, the sculptors fashioned misshapen creatures of barbarous power.
H. Gallet de Santerre, *Delos 24*, 1959, pls. 41–9.

45 *Gorgon mask c.* 700 B.C. painted terracotta 0·20 m.
Sacrificial pit, south of Court, Tiryns
Nauplion, Museum
Painted purple, red and black, equipped with real pigs' bristles over the mouth, this life-size mask worn in rituals is a stark reminder of the monstrous and irrational component in Archaic Greek art.
Karo, *Personality in Archaic Greek art*, 1948, pl. 3.

46 *Griffin c.* 650 B.C. bronze 0·265 m.
River Kladeos, Olympia
New York, Walter C. Baker Collection
Screaming fierceness of the mythical eagle-bird is ennobled and raised to monumental precision of the 'Daedalic' style. Three of these grandiose heads adorned the rim of a cauldron given to Zeus of Olympia.
U. Jantzen, *Griechische Greifenkessel*, 1955, pl. 30.

47 *Sphinx* 625 B.C. terracotta 0·335 m.
Kerameikos Cemetery, Athens
Athens, Kerameikos Museum
This sleepy-eyed sphinx represents the same tentative experimental style as the Delos lions (44). The large figurine supported a plate for incense.
Karo fig. 16.

48 *Sphinx of the Naxians* 580 B.C. marble 2·22 m.
Below Temple of Apollo, Delphi
Delphi, Museum
Set on a thirty-one-foot column, this emblem and present of the island of Naxos towered against the sky, a prophetic guardian of Apollo's shrine. The design insists upon the contrast of static volumes of face, body and legs and the curves of patterned hair, chest and wings.
P. Amandry, *La colonne des Naxiens*, 1959.

49 *Funerary sphinx* 530 B.C. marble 0·752 m.
From Attica
Boston, Museum of Fine Arts
The Early Archaic Delphian sphinx was firmly rooted to its base. This enchanting Late Archaic sphinx is poised, ready to spring. Animating life flows through wings, body, and spiralling tail, which echoes the

50   51★

52

53

54

55

56★

57

58

volutes of the base. She crowned a tall (*c.* 3·5 m.) funerary monument (*stele*).
Richter, *Gravestones* fig. 110.

50 *Colossal statue of a youth c.* 590 B.C. marble 3·05 m.
    Pit east of Temple of Poseidon, Sounion
    Athens, National Museum
    Young marble giants greeted the sailor from Cape Sounion as he entered the home stretch to Athens. Two basic intuitions of Greek art – tensed vitality and geometric structuring – are as yet disunited: the sculptor partly carves, partly maps an abstract concept of human form on to the rectangular block.
    Richter, *Kouroi* figs. 33–9.

51 KRITIOS? *Kouros* 485 B.C. marble 0·86 m.
    Acropolis, Athens
    Athens, Acropolis Museum
    Attributed (not conclusively) to Kritios, sculptor of the *Tyrannicides* (110), this masterly sculpture makes the crucial change from automatic Archaic to organic Classical concept. In frontal view the upper body remains immobile; the profile reveals the energy of stance based on the new 'natural' rhythm.
    Payne figs. 109–12. Richter, *Kouroi* fig. 564. Carpenter, *Art* pl. 3.

52 *Calf bearer* (*Rhonbos*) 560 B.C. marble 1·65 m.
    Southeast Acropolis (under Museum), Athens
    Athens, Acropolis Museum
    'The first Attic sculptor to whom working in three dimensions means working in the round' (H. Payne) created this masterpiece of interlocked unity of man and animal with its infectious good humour. The marble surfaces are of incredible beauty. The donor's name, '*Rhonbos ho polio*', is inscribed on base.
    Payne, pl. 2, A. Raubitschek, *Dedications from the Athenian Acropolis*, 1949, no. 59.

53 *Kouros c.* 540 B.C. marble 2·11 m.
    Attica
    Munich, Glyptothek
    Here at mid-point of the Archaic era, fleshed roundness of limbs prevails over abstract construction emphasized in early *kouroi* (50).

Disciplined human strength replaces other-worldly grandeur.
Richter, *Kouroi* fig. 393.

54 *Theseus* (*and Procrustes?*) 510–500 B.C. marble 0·63 m.
    East of Parthenon, Acropolis
    Athens, Acropolis Museum
    Theseus, boosted by democratic propaganda as mythical national hero of Athens, is battling an opponent, whose hand remains on Theseus' left shoulder. The artist strives to portray motion by twisting the upper part of the body; the rest of the figure remains close to the schematic *kouros* type.
    Schrader-Langlotz pl. 155. Payne pl. 106.

55 *Kouros c.* 500 B.C. marble 1·03 m.
    Leontini, Sicily (imported?)
    Syracuse, Museo Archeologico
    The great transition from Archaic to Classical sculpture took a multiplicity of ways. In this beautifully finished torso the softening and fluency of surface form is not as yet fully motivated by organic motion.
    Richter, *Kouroi* fig. 550.

56 *Horseman*, detail of 58

57 *Horseman c.* 550 B.C. bronze 0·10 m.
    Sanctuary of Zeus, Dodona, horseman 1870–80, horse 1956
    Athens. National Museum
    From wintry Dodona in northwest Greece come bronzes distinguished by cerulean patina. They were probably made in Corinth. Their sturdy simplicity is seen at its best in the engaging toy horse. It contrasts with Samian sophisticated charm (56, 58).
    S. Karousou, *Deutsche Beiträge zur Altertumswissenschaft*, 1960, fig. 6.

58 *Horseman* 530 B.C. bronze 0·195 m.
    Sanctuary of Hera, Samos
    Vathy (Samos), Museum
    Poetry, music and intellectual excitement flourished on the island of Samos under the tyrant Polycrates. Mobile, muscular, this slit-eyed boy infuses eager Ionian liveliness into the Archaic scheme of the prize-winning horseman.
    Buschor figs. 192, 199.

59★

60

61

63

64

65

66

67

62

59 *'Rampin' horseman c.* 560 B.C. marble head 0·35 m, torso 0·81 m.
Torso west of Erechtheum, Acropolis, Athens, 1886
Paris, Louvre (head), and Athens, Acropolis Museum (torso)
The earliest small marble statue of a horseman shows the sculptor wrestling with problems of complex grouping. Simple, large planes of face and torso are sharply broken. Head turned, the gay face is encased in Manneristic, ornamental hair, wreath and beard. Prize-winning nobleman or one of Dioscuri?
Payne pls. 11a–c. Lullies pl. 28.

60 *Horseman* 560 B.C. painted terracotta 0·35 m.
Lydian bazaar area, Sardis
Manisa, Archaeological Museum
A contemporary of 'Rampin' horseman, this piece was made in Lydia, a 'mixobarbarous' neighbour of Eastern Greeks. A body of inert amplitude, a glance of large-eyed wonder, soft forms, and broad pictorial effects make a striking contrast to the keen precision of the Greek marble-work.
Hanfmann, *8ᵉ Congrès International d'Archéologie Classique*, 1963, pl. 124:2.

61 *Basin supported by goddesses* 620 B.C. marble 1·26 m.
Sanctuary of Poseidon, Isthmia
Corinth, Museum
Archaic Greek art frequently used the human figure as support for vases and mirrors. This early type of sacred basin depends on semi-Oriental, Cypriote and Near Eastern models where Ishtar, goddess of love and battle, is often shown standing on a lion.
O. Broneer, *Hesperia*, 1958, pl. 11a.

62 GENELEOS *Family group c.* 560 B.C. marble H. Philippe 1·60 m., limestone base
Northern Road, Sanctuary of Hera, Samos
Vathy (Samos), Museum
This is the earliest family portrait group in Western sculpture. The frontal array on a common base was a revolutionary concept. Inscriptions announce: 'Geneleos made us'; 'I am . . . narche who dedicated it' and give names. Mother and children? from right: donoress; girl, lost; Philippe; Ornithe (not shown, *see* 64); boy, lost; Phileia (seated).
Buschor fig. 350. Jeffery, 329, 341.

63 *Figurine of a maiden c.* 570 B.C. bronze 0·27 m.
From a well, Sanctuary of Hera, Samos
Vathy (Samos), Museum
Earlier, less harmoniously designed than the Geneleos maidens, this little *kore* combines Egyptian solidity of body, garment and wig, with a big, joyous grin. Such may have been the style of the first large bronze statues of the famous sculptor, Theodorus, who learned bronze-casting in Egypt.
Society of Hellenic Studies, *Archaeological reports for 1963–4* fig. 28.

64 GENELEOS *Ornithe c.* 560 B.C. marble 1·68 m.
Sanctuary of Hera, Samos, part of a group (62)
Berlin, Staatliche Museen
The roundness of the body is sensed but understated, the softness and weight of garment just hinted at; the special charm of mid-Archaic Samian sculpture lies in the subdued revelation of simple volumes under the abstract beauty of linear patterns.
Buschor fig. 345. Blümel figs. 102–5.

65 *Priestess* 530 B.C. marble 0·55 m.
Column decoration, Temple of Apollo, Didyma
Berlin, Staatliche Museen
China and Medieval Flanders have been invoked to suggest the exotic strangeness of this priestly maiden. Much of this effect is due to native Anatolian veil and the slit eyes. The healthy face with high, angular cheeks, is good Archaic Greek. There is no gainsaying the child-like appeal of this very young, plumpish girl.
Blümel fig. 162. G. Gruben, *JdI*, 1963, fig. 9.

66 *Priestess*, profile view of 65

67 *'Peplos' kore* 540–530 B.C. marble 1·21 m.
Acropolis, Athens
Athens, Acropolis Museum
Much loved and photographed, the original statue surprises by its small size, red eyes and hair – that colour served as underpaint. It has been attributed by H. Payne and A. Rumpf to the master of the '*Rampin' horseman* (59). Subtle asymmetries enhance her irrepressible vitality and tectonic strength.
Payne pls. 29–33. Boardman fig. 64.

68

69

70*

71

72

73*

74

75

76

68 *Head of the 'Peplos' kore*, detail of 67
   Within the same Archaic formula as the exotic girl (65) the Attic sculptor achieves by slight rounding of eyes and mouth 'greater unity and plastic strength' (H. Payne), a face breathing radiant freshness of an early morning.

69 *The 'Sphinx' kore c.* 500 B.C. marble 0·92 m.
   Southwest of Parthenon, Acropolis, Athens
   Athens, Acropolis Museum
   The *'Mona Lisa'* of Archaic art owes her nickname to her enigmatic expression, which glides from the gaiety of Archaic maidens to the pensive solemnity of Early Classic divinities. 'In form and spirit her sculptor strove to discover what is essentially feminine' (H. Payne).
   Payne pls. 75–8. Schrader-Langlotz pl. 62.

70 *Seated priestly ruler* 570 B.C. marble 1·55 m.
   Sacred Road to Sanctuary of Apollo, Didyma
   London, British Museum
   Early travellers saw some sixty statues flanking the road to the Oracle of Apollo. This, the earliest preserved, is uncompromising in making heavy rotund volumes express dignity and repose. He is probably one of the priestly clan of Branchidai, who supervised the sanctuary.
   Pryce I:1, pl. 6.

71 *Aeakes?* 540 B.C. marble 1·51 m.
   Reused in Byzantine wall, Tigani, Samos
   Tigani, Museum
   Inscribed 'Aeakes, son of Bryson, dedicated to Hera the owed booty in accord with his office as head of State.' The sculptor achieves monumentality by co-ordinating the large curves of body and garment with the verticals and horizontals of the throne, which is adorned with sphinxes.
   Buschor figs. 141–3 (statue of Hera). Jeffery, 330.

72 *Seated man* 530–520 B.C. marble 1·08 m.
   Kerameikos Cemetery, Athens
   Athens, Kerameikos Museum
   Seated at the foot of a burial mound, the statue commemorated an important Athenian. Precision and clarity in designing body and garment are typically Attic, and contrast with the weightiness of his Ionian contemporary (71).
   Karo pl. 20. C. Karousos, *Aristodikos*, 1961, 63.

73 *Proteus?* 550 B.C. painted limestone 0·71 m.
   Pediment of a large temple, Acropolis, Athens
   Athens, Acropolis Museum
   Attic limestone was more easily cut than marble and took colour well. The three-bodied *daimon* is a group of great size and complexity. Much of the colour survives: blue hair and beard, yellow flesh, red and black feathers and scales. Here for once Archaic sculpture is good-naturedly humorous.
   Boardman fig. 68. Lullies pls. I, II (colour).

74 *Persephone?* 470 B.C. marble 1·51 m.
   Sanctuary, Via Abruzzi, Tarentum
   Berlin, Staatliche Museen
   With hieratic intent the sculptor made posture and garment Archaic, yet the fullness of body, the motion of arms and folds, and the splendidly serene head reveal the new concept of Early Classic divinity. It is perhaps the only surviving cult statue of that revolutionary age.
   Langlotz pls. 50ff. Blümel, 55–8.

75 *A portrait?* 540–530 B.C. marble 0·23 m.
   Formerly Sabouroff Collection
   Berlin, Staatliche Museen
   The strange roughened hair-cap and moustache – which some think was covered with stucco – may be accidental, but the enigmatic, hovering smile is individual. Tensed by strong modelling, the lucent, greenish surface of the face is of breathtaking beauty.
   Blümel pls. 16–19. Payne, 37.

76 *Winged youth* 650 B.C. terracotta 0·14 m.
   Sanctuary of Hera, Argos
   Athens, National Museum
   Carefully disposed within the rectangular frame, the striding youth holds a spiralling plant, symbolic of vegetative life. The projecting, frontal head is icon-like in its supernatural stare. Some have thought him Dionysos, god of wine; a superb example of relief in the earliest monumental, 'Daedalic' style.
   Matz pl. 92. C. Waldstein, *Argive Heraeum* 2, 1905, pl. 49:1.

79*

82

84

83

85

77

78

80

81

77 *Owl c.* 650 B.C. painted terracotta (vase) 0·052 m.
Made in Corinth
Paris, Louvre
A master of the Protocorinthian school, renowned for its miniaturistic vase-painting, has unified simple rotund body and impeccably ornamental wings to create a convincingly alive, quizzical owl. The little bird is also a perfume flask.
Payne, *Protokorinthische* pl. 25; *Necrocorinthia*, 1931, pl. 44:4.

78 *Gorgon from the Temple of Artemis* 580 B.C. limestone 2·79 m.
West pediment, Temple of Artemis, Korkyra (Corfu)
Korkyra, Museum
In a bold bid to design a large sculptured stone pediment, a great sculptor from Corinth displayed a huge Gorgon, half apotropaic mask, half mighty runner, as she gives birth to hero Chrysaor (right) and Pegasus, flanked by heraldic leopards and small narrative groups (79). The method is enumerative, epical; the style, of Early Archaic grandeur.
Lullies pl. 17. Rodenwaldt, *Korkyra* 2, 1939, pl. 14.

79 *West pediment* 580 B.C. limestone W. 22·16 m.
Temple of Artemis, Korkyra
Korkyra, Museum
Three slayings: Gorgon-Medusa, giving life in death (78); Priam slain by Neoptolemos, dead Trojan (left); Zeus slaying giant, dead giant (right): the gods' purpose comes to pass. The huge beasts submit to the will of the goddess, who is inside the temple. The content is unified by 'protoabstract' speculation found also in Early Greek poetry, the design by formal symmetry.
Rodenwaldt, *Korkyra* 2, 1939, pl. 2c. Lullies pls. 16–19.

80 *Flying Victory (Nike)* 550 B.C. marble 0·90 m.
Sanctuary of Artemis, Delos
Athens, National Museum
Temple acroterion or votive? The controversy is still unresolved. Round-faced, smiling Victory thrusts her arms into space; in a great innovation folds sweep down over her legs. Her large wings are broken behind her shoulders. Poised against the Greek sky this first winged Victory inaugurated a theme which reverberated through European sculpture all the way to Rodin's *La Défense* (*see* viii, 118, 234).
Richter, *Sculpture* fig. 77. Marcadé, 2, 21.

81 *Gorgon* 560 B.C. painted terracotta 0·56 m.
Old Temple of Athena?, Syracuse
Syracuse, Museo Archeologico
The Gorgon clutches Pegasus, whom she brought forth when Perseus killed her. The small, much-restored relief makes effective play with colour of wings and garment, but its compact design and intentional frightfulness are no match for the magnificent swing and joyous vitality of the Korkyra *Gorgon* (78).
Langlotz colour pl. 1. Boardman fig. 48.

82 *The Trojan Horse* 675–650 B.C. ceramic H. of vase 1·33 m.
Near harbour, in a grave, Mykonos
Mykonos, Museum
On this burial jar the sculptor-potter tried to rival epic poets in historic narration. His formulaic vocabulary consists of repeated units stamped with moulds. Achaean heroes look out of the horse's neck like passengers in a train.
Boardman fig. 47. M. Ervin, *Deltion*, 1963, pl. 18.

83 *Dead man torn by vulture* 680 B.C. ceramic fragment 0·165 m.
Island of Tenos
Athens, National Museum
'A meal for vultures', like the Achaeans in the sombre opening of the *Iliad*: a few twists suffice to transform the traditional schematic man of Geometric style into an image of stark pathos. This is part of large jar with bands of narrative relief.
Matz pl. 281b.

84 *Monument in form of Ionic temple* 550 B.C. marble 0·62 m.
Reused in synagogue, Sardis
Manisa, Museum
Mutilated, difficult to photograph because of very shallow relief, the monument shows a goddess in her temple between two rising snakes: eighteen panels portray priestesses, sileni, lions, myths: their arrangement over the entire height of the wall reveals a totally novel solution in combining architecture and sculpture.
Hanfmann, *Archaeology*, 1966, 93, fig. 4.

85 *Frieze of horsemen* 640 B.C. limestone 0·84 m.
Temple A, Prinias, Crete
Heraklion, Museum

311

88

90

91*

92

86

89

93

87

In small terracotta reliefs (76) sculptors gained experience of relief compositions which could be enlarged into monumental stone sculpture. The parade of emphatically vertical, spear-swinging knights is perhaps the earliest frieze of stone known on a Greek temple. Matz pl. 86. Demargne fig. 456.

86 *Heracles slaying centaurs* 540 B.C. trachyte 0·82 m.
Frieze, Temple of Athena, Assos
Boston, Museum of Fine Arts
Much has happened to the temple frieze since the upright horsemen of Prinias (85). The clear direction, the echoing running figures are diversified by turn of head and gestures of arms. Eager Heracles, stampeding centaurs and astonished host Pholos are neatly characterized. Caskey no. 7.

87 *Battle between Greeks and Trojans* 530–525 B.C. marble *c.* 0·65 m.
East frieze, right half, Treasury of Siphnos, Delphi
Delphi, Museum
Movement is semi-abstract, and compositional schemes heraldic. The novelty lies in the three-dimensional essays of the superb horse teams, in the eloquent placing of an 'end figure' on the right, and of the pathetic dead in centre. Protagonists: Hector, Aeneas (left) – Menelaos (right).

88 *Battle of gods (Heracles and Cybele) and giants* 530–525 B.C. marble 0·65 m.
North frieze: Heracles, Cybele, Apollo, Artemis (on right), Treasury of Siphnos, Delphi
Delphi, Museum
The friezes are dense with slightly flattened but plastic figures, interwoven in heavy-gaited rhythm. For the first time each side of the building is given a unified subject and composed as a unit; two stories of war (Troy; Gods and Giants); two stories of love (Elopement; Judgement of Paris). On the shield of giant who fights Apollo, incomplete signature of the designer of the north and east friezes; his name is lost. The treasury is firmly dated before 525 B.C., when Samians seized Siphnos. Marcadé, I, 119. Lullies pls. 48–55.

89 *Cybele's lions fighting giants*, detail of 88
Heracles and the Asiatic Mother of Gods and her lions fight helmeted giants. The Late Archaic skill in relating descriptive decorative detail to

strong rounded volume was never more strikingly displayed, nor marble more delicately carved.

90 *Crater* 510 B.C. bronze 1·64 m.
Mound burial, Vix, near Chatillon
Chatillon-sur-Seine, Museum
Found in the grave of a Celtic princess, the gigantic vessel treats sculptural decoration in architectural manner. The frieze is placed 'under roof', the Gorgons and lions of the handles at the edges, like acroteria on a temple.
R. Joffroy, *Le trésor de Vix*, 1954.

91 *Warrior and chariot*, detail of 90 relief 0·14 m.
Spartan warriors stride with measured step between heroic chariots. The groups repeat; careful spacing and upright stance work for decorative containment. Yet, in modelling of body, horses and men are closer to Classical naturalness than their lively counterparts in Delphi (87).

92 *Heracles and the Kerkopes* 560 B.C. sandstone 0·78 m.
Treasury, Heraion of Lucania, Foce del Sele
Paestum, Museum
Drastic, humorous story-telling triumphs in the metope made by a provincial sculptor from the Greek colony of Poseidonia (Paestum). The twin sprites Kerkopes had plagued Heracles until he suspended them head down from a pole.
Langlotz pl. 11.

93 *Boxer* (fragment) 550 B.C. marble 0·23 m.
Re-used in wall built by Themistocles in Athens, 478 B.C.
Athens, Kerameikos Museum
The boxer raises his hand in victory. The round head is divided into three balanced areas. The nose is big, a sign of character. In a world apart, he is smiling to himself; compare the grimly determined Classical, the battered but defiant Hellenistic boxers (169, 246).
Richter, *Gravestones* fig. 92.

94 *Child and mother's hand* c. 530 B.C. marble 0·385 m.
Anavysos
Athens, National Museum

94

95★

96★

97

98

99

100

101

Because of its reliance on externalized action and formulaic gesture, Archaic art was limited in exploring emotional relationships. Yet the head of the diminutive adult becomes an eloquent image of tenderness in the sinuous but assuring grasp of the mother's hand.

Richter, *Gravestones* fig. 152. Classical version of similar theme (149).

95 *Youth (athletic victor?) c.* 480 B.C. marble 1·10 m.
Sanctuary near River Akragas (S. Biagio)
Agrigento, Museo Civico
Beautifully finished, this youth is another (51, 55), more austere witness for that unique moment in the history of sculpture when the human body began to live and speak. With gentle swelling of muscles and slow rise of the arms, the statue opens itself to the world.
Langlotz fig. 54.

CLASSICAL GREEK SCULPTURE

96 *Apollo* 460 B.C. marble 3·35 m.
West pediment, Temple of Zeus, Olympia
Olympia, Museum
With commanding gesture, Apollo appears among the fighting Greeks and centaurs. The splendour of his firm, upright body was originally set off by a purple cloak. This vision of inexorable avenger of right is of Aeschylean grandeur.
Rodenwaldt, *Olympia*, 1936, fig. 44.

97 *Athena, Heracles and Atlas* (not shown) *c.* 460 B.C. marble 1·60 m.
Metope over the entrance to inner shrine, Temple of Zeus, Olympia
Olympia, Museum
In one of the twelve deeds required to achieve immortality Heracles, the first Olympic victor, obtains the apples of the Hesperides from King Atlas, whom he relieves in supporting the heavens. Athena assists. Nobility of concept and pure beauty of marble make this a high point in the sequence of twelve metopes.
Rodenwaldt, *Olympia*, 1936, fig. 105. Lullies pl. 107.

98 *Athena looking at Stymphalid Birds c.* 460 B.C. marble 1·60 m.
Metope, Temple of Zeus, Olympia
Olympia, Museum
In the metopes depicting the biography of Heracles, muscle-bursting action alternates with scenes where accent is on mood. Seated barefoot on a rock, 'like a village girl', Athena smiles at the trophy which Heracles presents. The birds are lost.
Rodenwaldt, *Olympia*, 1936, pl. 67.

99 *Charioteer* 477 B.C. bronze, onyx inlay (eyes) 1·80 m.
North of the Temple of Apollo, Delphi, with fragments of chariot, 1896
Delphi, Museum
Votive of King Polyzalos of Gela for victory in chariot race. In this most solemn of victory monuments the slight motion of upper body and head, the tensing of neck and arm, the breathing mouth, animate the columnar entity with subdued life and new sense of freedom. Masterly curves rise through garment and shoulders to the superlative calm of the skull. As he concentrates on his parade drive, the charioteer is alone in that proud immortality to which god-given victory elevates man.
Lullies pls. 98–100. F. Chamoux, *L'Aurige*, 1955.

100 *Oinomaos and Sterope?* 460 B.C. marble *c.* 3·025 m.
East pediment, Temple of Zeus, Olympia
Olympia, Museum
In harshly vertical array two couples flanked Zeus. The spectator knew the outcome of the impending drama. Grim Oinomaos, who used to slay his daughter's suitors, will himself be slain. Most scholars consider the majestic woman Sterope, his wife; but others Hippodameia, his daughter.
Lullies pls. 110ff.

101 *Head of Athena*, detail of 98
The art of Olympia is distinguished by large forms, full of experimental stress and strain in pediments, softened, more harmonious in metopes. Bending of head, attentive glance, slight pursing of lips, serve to characterize Athena and relate her to Heracles in a common concern.
Rodenwaldt, *Olympia*, 1936, pl. 70.

102

103

105   106

107*

108

109*

110

102 *Head of the charioteer*, detail of 99
In pioneering departure, the side locks exploit fluidity of casting to modulate the austere outline with plastic movement. The expression of the charioteer changes with play of light in the translucent onyx pupils, a revolutionary optic device to symbolize the newly discovered inner light of the soul.

103 *Panathenaic procession* (*marshal and maidens*) 440–438 B.C. marble 1·06 m.
East frieze, Parthenon, Acropolis, Athens
Paris, Louvre
What was promised in the *Charioteer* is fulfilled. Columnar statues walk, united by a slow but seemingly natural rhythm. The flow of motion is smoother, the physical presence of draped, rounded bodies more pervasive, the mood of lofty piety softened from pride to thoughtful acceptance.
Corbett fig. 12. Picard 2:1, fig. 182.

104 *Young cavalryman* 440–438 B.C. marble *c.* 0·60 m.
West end of north frieze, Group XLII, Parthenon, Acropolis, Athens
London, British Museum
The design of the Parthenon frieze was a marvel; the execution varied. The eloquent unfolding of boyish beauty against the heaving background of restless horses is the designer's. Caressing the marble, the executing sculptor emphasized the quick, springy contours of body, the soft dreaminess of head.
Yalouris pl. 11. A. Michaelis, *Der Parthenon*, 1870, pl. 13.

105 *Funerary stele* ('*Cat Stele*') *c.* 410 B.C. marble 1·09 m.
From Salamis?
Athens, National Museum
The farewell gesture of the noble youth, radiantly pure in white marble, clashes with a rising ladder of things he left behind: servant-boy, cat, bird-cage. One of the Parthenon sculptors strives to fit the young *polis* hero into the frame of domestic intimacy required for a family memorial.
Lullies fig. 182.

106 *Funerary stele of a warrior* 420 B.C. marble 1·838 m.
Megara
Worcester, Mass., Art Museum

In this fine funerary relief the 'Polykleitan stance' receives a more specific connotation: the dead is real yet remote, subject to time yet timeless. There is hidden tension between the optic reality of foreshortening in leg and shield and the neutral, stony background.
H. Diepolder, *Die attischen Grabreliefs*, 1931, fig. 3.

107 POLYKLEITOS *Doryphoros* original *c.* 450 B.C., modern reconstruction bronze 1·99 m.
Munich, University
In this statue Polykleitos illustrated his dogma that sculpture is an aesthetic problem, to be solved by proportional geometry applied to a generalized scheme of motion. His curve of motion derives from the effects of pull and counter-pull upon skeletal structure. It results in a timeless yet lifelike stance.
Carpenter, *Sculpture* pl. 13. Pollitt, 88.

108 *Heracles c.* 500 B.C. bronze 0·127 m.
Sanctuary of Hera, Perachora, near Corinth
Athens, National Museum
Swinging a club, bow in hand, Heracles advances deliberately, irresistibly – a far cry from the eager angularity of the Assos frieze (86). The stance implies that he will pivot. Though small, the figurine is fine enough to illustrate an early stage of Classical experiments in balanced motion.
Payne, *Perachora* 1, 1940, pl. 45.

109 *Zeus or Poseidon?* 460 B.C. bronze 2·09 m.
From Roman shipwreck off Cape Artemision, Euboea
Athens, National Museum
The great Greek original bronze statue of Early Classical Age arose from the sea in 1926. The balanced grandeur of motion renders the essence of Early Classic divinity. The head is thoughtful but serene, uninvolved in the action of the body.
Lullies pls. 130–32. Picard 2:1, pls. 14 ff.

110 KRITIOS and NESIOTES *Aristogeiton* original 477 B.C., Roman copy marble 1·95 m.
Original bronze, part of *Tyrannicides*, Agora, Athens
Rome, Palazzo Conservatori

111   112   113   114   115★   116   117   118★

In 514 B.C. the tyrant Hipparchos was slain by Harmodios and Aristogeiton. Roman copies have been combined to reconstitute an older (shown) and a younger tyrant slayer (not shown). The grand motion of Olympian immortals was bestowed upon new immortals of democracy. How the two statues were grouped is controversial.
Picard 2:1, 10. H. Thompson, *The Athenian Agora*, 1962, 70.

111 *Heracles and the Cretan bull c.* 460 B.C. marble 1·60 m.
Metope, western front of cella, Temple of Zeus, Olympia
Paris, Louvre, and Olympia, Museum (head of bull, smaller parts)
Violent motion contained in a tectonic frame was the problem upon which the experimentalist sculptors of Olympia seized with intense concentration. The novel, centripetal design of 'two mighty diagonals which signify the elemental force of conflict' (Rodenwaldt) is rendered with bursting power in spite of semi-linear detail.
Rodenwaldt, *Olympia*, 1936, fig. 72. Picard 2:1, fig. 88.

112 *Centaur triumphant* 442 B.C. marble 1·34 m.
Metope XXVIII, south side of Parthenon, Athens
London, British Museum
Rising in triumph, the broad-muscled centaur rides over the broken, slender youth. With amazing inventiveness the designer displayed some twenty variations of the duel between man and monster in masterly changes of pace and balance.
Corbett fig. 3. Lullies pl. 142.

113 *Greek and Amazon* original 438 B.C. Roman copy *c.* A.D. 150 marble 0·90 m.
From ancient shipwreck in Piraeus
Piraeus, Museum
Almost six centuries after Phidias the shield of the Parthenon statue (141, 153) was still copied in 'abstracts' for Roman art lovers. Despite cold ineptness of copyist, the reliefs show a landscape setting more continuous and an action more passionate than those of other Parthenon sculptures.
W. Fuchs, *Die Vorbilder der neuattischen Reliefs*, 1958, pl. 34.

114 MYRON *Discus-thrower* original *c.* 440 B.C. modern reconstruction
Rome, Museo Nazionale delle Terme

Recomposed from casts taken of the body of a Roman copy in the Vatican and the head from the statue (115), then cast in bronze. Falsified twice – bronze into marble, marble into bronze – the reconstruction makes one vital point: how much the motion gains without the dragging support which Roman copyists introduced to prevent the legs from breaking.
Richter, *Sculpture* figs. 568–82. Carpenter, *Sculpture* pl. 9.

115 MYRON *Discus-thrower* original *c.* 440 B.C. Roman copy marble 1·25 m.
Marble copy, formerly Lancelotti Collection, Rome
Rome, Museo Nazionale delle Terme
Myron built his design round a half-circle crossed by an 'S'-curve. The action moved only sideways within a shallow space, but as a convincing symbol of rapid motion the concept was revolutionary for sculpture in the round. Technically, the original of bronze with its small areas of support was almost as venturesome as Cellini's *Perseus*.

116 *Discus-thrower* 450–430 B.C. bronze 0·153 m.
Sanctuary of the Kabiros, Thebes
Athens, National Museum
For Myron (114) a discus-thrower was whirling motion. This joyful athlete is sturdily poised, upright; he holds the discus aloft as if victory were already his. Inscribed: '*Kabiro*' ('to the Kabiros').
G. Bruns, *Neue Ausgrabungen im Mittelmeergebiet*, 1959, 246, fig. 8.

117 *Hephaistos c.* 460 B.C. bronze 0·215 m.
Perhaps from Attica
Washington, D.C., Dumbarton Oaks Collection
Pivoting as he strides, the god or hero swings from the shoulders, smiling a gleeful smile not devoid of malice. No sculpture can rival this work in making the body so completely a vehicle of singing rhythm. The roughened 'Impressionistic' surface is due to corrosion.
Richter, *Dumbarton Oaks* pl. 9.

118 PAIONIOS OF MENDE *Nike (Victory) c.* 440 B.C. marble 2·16 m.
Pedestal in Altis, Olympia
Olympia, Museum (statue) (★Reconstruction shown above)
Between the entrance into the Sanctuary and the entrance to the Temple of Zeus stand the remains of a triangular marble pedestal,

315

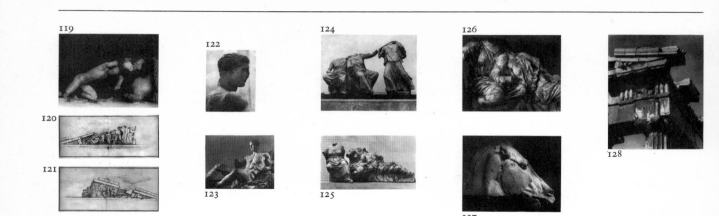

originally thirty feet high. Captured shields were attached to it. Inscribed: 'The Messenians and Naupaktians gave to Olympian Zeus the tithe of booty taken from their enemies. Paionios of Mende made [the statue of Nike] and won the prize for having made the acroteria above the temple [of Zeus].' The battle, often identified as that of Sphakteria (424 B.C.), cannot be safely determined. The mighty statue has lost face, forearms, wings, and the colouring which heightened the illusion of Victory's descent from the sky.
Rodenwaldt, *Olympia*, 1936, fig. 29, pl. 84. Carpenter, *Sculpture* pl. 24. Lullies pl. 178.

119 *Youth battling a centaur c.* 460 B.C. marble original W. of group 4·25 m.
West pediment, Temple of Zeus, Olympia
Olympia, Museum
Archaic pediments were composed in separate units. The designer of the Early Classic pediment created a continuous pattern of violent physical action. One of his most dynamic inventions is the youth forcing down a centaur; the boy's bulging muscles, however, are still 'mapped' and stationary.
Rodenwaldt, *Olympia*, 1936, pl. 58.

120 and 121 ANONYMOUS FLEMISH DRAUGHTSMAN *East pediment of the Parthenon* 1674
Paris, Bibliothèque Nationale
Passing through Athens with the French Embassy staff a Baroque draughtsman sketched the Parthenon sculptures. The central group, Athena's birth from head of Zeus, was already lost. Only an approximate idea of this composition can be gained from preserved fragments, statue beddings in the pediment, and reflections in Roman reliefs.
Brommer pl. 2. Carpenter, *Hesperia* Suppl. 8, 1949.

122 *Head of Dionysos?* detail of 123

123 *Dionysos?* 437–432 B.C. marble 1·30 m.
Figure 'D' from east pediment of the Parthenon, Athens
London, British Museum
The only pedimental figure which retains its head, this young god or hero has been variously identified. He reclines on an animal skin and turns towards the rising sun. Though the surface is battered, the slow

unfolding of life in the body and the prophetic, far-away look on the face are of haunting majesty.
Brommer pl. 27. Haynes fig. 24.

124 *Demeter, Kore and messenger* 437–432 B.C. marble H. of 'G' 1·73 m.
Figures 'E', 'F', 'G' from east pediment of the Parthenon, Athens
London, British Museum
The two goddesses seated on chests are probably goddesses of holy fertility rites of Eleusis; the messenger is controversial (Iris, Hebe, Artemis, Eleithyia?). No matter – the sense of ebbing motion, of communication made and received, of bodies larger than life circumscribed by heavy eloquence of folds remains miraculous.
Brommer pl. 22. Yalouris pls. 3–6.

125 *Hestia?, Dione?, Aphrodite* 437–432 B.C. marble H. of 'K' 1·34 m.
Figures 'K', 'L', 'M' from east pediment of the Parthenon, Athens
London, British Museum
The right half of the pediment relates the passing of the night. Aphrodite, cosmic goddess of love, begins to stir in her dreams. The rhythm of plastic forms is completely congruent with natural movement of the two bodies; folds circle and break like waves. Compared to Aphrodite's massive, relaxed grandeur, Michelangelo's *Night* seems uneasy and strained.
Brommer pl. 45. Picard 2:1, 482. Rodenwaldt, *Acropolis*, 1936, fig. 29.

126 *Dione? and Aphrodite*, detail of 125
Acute analysis of drapery, Carpenter, *Sculpture* 140.

127 *Horse-head from Selene's chariot* 437–432 B.C. marble L. 0·82 m.
Figure 'O' from east pediment of the Parthenon, Athens
London, British Museum
Four horse-heads served to describe the teams of the sun god and moon goddess, one rising, the other sinking into the sea. Pulsating with untamed, fiery life, this head seemed to Goethe to sum up the prototypical quintessence of horse as intended by a pantheistic nature.
Corbett pl. 40. Brommer pls. 56–60.

128 *Northeast corner of the Parthenon* marble, outer horse 0·92 m.
Athens, Acropolis

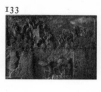

The sculptures of the Parthenon gained their ultimate artistic effect from contrast with the framework of architecture and from dramatic light and shade bestowed by the sun. The splendid lion-head both terminates and transcends the geometric end of the roof. The near horse-head is a cast of 127. The metope in shade showed the chariot of the Sun.
Picard 2:1, fig. 173 (Sun). Brommer, *Giebel* pl. 33.

129 *Kekrops and daughter*, detail of 131

130 *River god or hero?* 437–432 B.C. marble L. 1·56 m.
Figure 'A' from north corner of west pediment of the Parthenon, Athens
London, British Museum
The recumbent figure, traditional in pedimental corners, is more fluid, less structured than *Dionysos* (123). Often identified as the Attic river, Ilissos, it may represent one of the numerous ancestral heroes worshipped on the Acropolis.
Brommer pls. 81–4. Haynes fig. 19.

131 *Kekrops and daughter* 437–432 B.C. marble H. of 'C' 1·37 m.
Figures 'B', 'C', north wing of west pediment
Athens, Parthenon.
Seen in its rightful place, this group vibrates with intensive life, a masterly combination of motion and repose. A snake between the legs of the man identifies Kekrops, snake-legged king buried under the Maidens' Porch of the Erechtheum; the maiden seeking refuge is probably his daughter.
Brommer pl. 85. Rodenwaldt, *Acropolis*, 1936, pl. 21.

132 *Amphitrite* 437–432 B.C. marble 1·10 m.
Figure 'O' from west pediment of the Parthenon, Athens
London, British Museum
Poseidon's chariot horses reared high; the female charioteer, probably Poseidon's wife, Amphitrite, strains mightily to hold the team. The execution is somewhat dry; the composition was magnificent, yet another example of the designer-sculptor's inexhaustibly rich vision of the human body in motion.
Brommer, *Giebel* pl. 40, with newly added fragment of right leg.

133 *Siege of Troy?* c. 400 B.C. limestone 1·20 m.
Internal western wall, Heroon of Gölbasi-Trysa, Lycia
Vienna, Kunsthistorisches Museum
This strange sepulchral monument for a barbarian ruler is the only detailed sculptural rendering of ambitious narrative compositions which featured architectural settings and relatively small figures. Presumably this tradition was developed in lost Classical paintings.
Picard 2:2, fig. 357. F. Eichler, *Die Reliefs von Gjölbaschi-Trysa*, 1950, pl. 18.

134 *Chariot* c. 438 B.C. marble 0·96 m.
South frieze of the Parthenon, Athens
London, British Museum
The dashing chariot and rearing horse help visualize the central composition of the west pediment (v). There is growing awareness of optical effects in superposition of bodies crossed by the receding shield.
Rodenwaldt, *Acropolis*, 1936, 38.

135 *Assembly of gods* c. 420 B.C. marble 0·448 m. (frieze)
Athens, Temple of Athena Nike, Acropolis, east frieze
The small Ionic Temple of Athena-Victory is a jewel of dainty precision. Three friezes showed battle scenes; the east frieze makes the assembly of gods consciously statuesque, many of them isolated in near frontality.
Rodenwaldt, *Acropolis*, 1936, pls. 69–73.

136 *Head of Apollo* 460–450 B.C. bronze 0·36 m.
Sanctuary of Apollo?, Tamassos, Cyprus
London, British Museum
One imagines this stern head colossal; actually it belonged to a statue only half life-size. It served as a cult image in Oriental Cyprus, but its style, more intellectual in concept, richer in form than Olympia's *Apollo* (96) points to Athens at the time of Phidias' youth.
J. Chittenden, *Greek Art*, 1946, pl. 64.

137 *Asklepios c.* 380 B.C. marble 0·64 m.
Sanctuary of Asklepios, Epidauros
Athens, National Museum

137

138

139

140

141

142

143

144

The majestic but benevolent 'father-image' created by Phidias was quickly adopted for other divinities. In a typical Late Classical interpretation, relaxed posture, softened forms, and inviting gesture make the god of healing accessible and humane.

Richter, *Sculpture* fig. 714, attributes it to the sculptor Timotheos.

138 PHIDIAS *Head of Zeus of Olympia c.* 430 B.C. on coin of Elis bronze 0·03 m.
Struck under Hadrian A.D. 133
Berlin, Staatliche Museen
The Roman coins give more detail for the head than the body (139) of the Phidian *Zeus*. One divines its formal clarity in the simple outline and the large divisions of the long-locked head.
J. Liegle, *Der Zeus des Phidias*, 1952, pl. 1.

139 PHIDIAS *Zeus of Olympia c.* 430 B.C. on coin of Elis bronze 0·03 m.
Struck under Hadrian
Florence, Museo Archeologico
No statue was more admired in Antiquity than the colossal gold and ivory *Zeus* by Phidias. The poet Callimachus worked its dimensions into a teasing poem; the touristic guide Pausanias described it in detail (V:11, 3). The sketchy coin is the only recognized authority for the general appearance.
Picard 2:1, fig. 152. F. Imhoof-Blumer, *Ancient Coins*, 1964, pl. P:xx-xxi.

140 *Head of Zeus c.* 350 B.C. marble 0·48 m.
Sanctuary of Carian Zeus, Mylasa
Boston, Museum of Fine Arts
Closer in time and type to the Phidian *Zeus*, the over life-sized head features the soft form and expression, the time-conscious 'breathing' effect, the *sfumato* surface which represent the apogee of Late Classical style. The work is by one of the sculptors of the Mausoleum.
Caskey no. 25.

141 PHIDIAS *Athena Parthenos* original *c.* 438 B.C. Hellenistic copy *c.* 160 B.C. marble 3·10 m.
Centre of Main Hall, Royal Library, Pergamon
Berlin, Staatliche Museen (Pergamon Museum)
The Hadrianic *Athena Parthenos* was an 'erudite work', striving to be faithful to a revered original. A creative adaptation rather than a copy, the dynamic *Athena* which presided over the famous Royal Library of Pergamon infused Phidian majesty with momentary vitality of the Hellenistic Age.
Schober fig. 89. Picard 2:1, fig. 159

142 PHIDIAS *Athena Parthenos* original *c.* 438 B.C. Roman copy *c.* A.D. 130 marble 1·045 m.
North of Varvakion, Athens, 1880
Athens, National Museum
The colossal chryselephantine image in the Parthenon towered some forty feet. The copyist tried to convey Athena's three-dimensional effect and render her major attributes as precisely as reduction to one-twelfth and translation into marble would permit. He indicated some colouristic effects of the original (yellow and gold hair, black pupil). Coldly mechanical, partly from Hadrianic Classicism, partly from lack of plastic sensibility, this is the most reliable copy for general design.
W. H. Schuchardt, *Antike Plastik*, 2:3 1963, pl. 63. Richter, *Sculpture* fig. 599.

143 *Aphrodite* 460–450 B.C. bronze 0·107 m.
Possibly from Epidauros
Cambridge, Mass., Fogg Art Museum, Harvard University
The little figurine is an unusual variant of the great columnar statues of Early Classical goddesses. Long curves of the garment circle round the body, leaving exposed a lean shoulder and a small breast. The arms are sharply angled. The artist saw Aphrodite not as a soft servant of love, but as an austere, vengeful power.
Hanfmann, *AJA*, 1962, pls. 73 ff.

144 *Artemis* 438 B.C. marble *c.* 0·61 m.
Detail from east frieze of the Parthenon, Acropolis, Athens
Athens, Acropolis Museum
Over the entrance to the temple twelve Olympian gods flanked the ritual folding of Athena's cloak and received the procession of Athenians. The pure beauty of Artemis in the golden marble is no more stone, nor yet flesh. With casual grip Artemis pulls up the slipping garment – an effect which betrays the sculptor's nascent interest in specifically feminine charm.
Corbett pl. 12 (position in frieze). Lullies pl. 157.

145   146   147   148   149   150   151*   152

145 *Head of a woman* 420–410 B.C. marble 0·27 m.
From Destruction of Troy, west pediment, Temple of Hera, Argos
Athens, National Museum
The theorist and 'constructivist', Polykleitos, made the image for the Temple of Hera. We do not know who made the pedimental sculptures. The fine head of a goddess or heroine, leaner, lower-browed than Parthenonian women, has an energetic vigour which points towards heroic dynamism of Late Classical sculpture.
Richter, *Sculpture* fig. 165. C. Waldstein, *Argive Heraeum*, 1902, pl. 36.

146 *'Caryatid' maiden* 420 B.C. marble 2·30 m.
South porch of Erechtheum, Acropolis, Athens
London, British Museum
This and the next two plates illustrate a famous invention of the High Classical period and its impact upon Roman Classicism. Although the Greeks compared the temple to the human body and columns to maidens, such literal humanization was rare. Called only 'maidens' in building inscription of 409 B.C., they walked eternally in solemn ritual for the mythical King Kekrops who was buried supposedly underneath the porch.
J. M. Paton, *The Erechtheum*, 1927, pl. 38. Picard 2:2, fig. 300.

147 *Caryatid*, Roman copy of *Erechtheum maiden* 10–4 B.C. marble
Attic of the side colonnades, Forum of Augustus, Rome
Rome, reconstructed in Loggia of the Knights of Rhodes
In a programmatic 'quotation' which makes Classical Greek art part of his ideal Roman state the emperor Augustus introduced copies of Erechtheum maidens into his Forum. Form and function changes as the maidens march above representations of Roman triumphators from Aeneas to Augustus.
E. Nash, *Pictorial dictionary*, 1961, fig. 496. D. Strong fig. 40.

148 *Erechtheum maiden*, copy *c.* A.D. 125 marble
Tivoli, Canopus, Hadrian's Villa
For emperor-architect Hadrian, Classical art was part of a cosmopolitan culture and of his private romantic dreams. To realize them he designed vast architectural landscapes adorned with Egyptian and Greek statuary and gave them names of famous sites he had visited.
Hanfmann, *Roman* colour pl. 1. Rowland fig. 44.

149 *Funerary stele of Ampharete* 420 B.C. marble 1·20 m.
Kerameikos Cemetery, Athens
Athens, Kerameikos Museum
'Beloved child of my daughter, as I used to hold you on my knees when we saw the rays of the sun – so I hold you now, dead the dead.' The immortal goddess (148) has become a mortal grandmother. Instead of the glory of the *polis*, human affection in the family claims immortality through beautiful memory.
Karo pl. 28.

150 DEXAMENES OF CHIOS *Portrait of a man* 420 B.C. scaraboid jasper 0·02 m.
Tomb at Kara, Attica
Boston, Museum of Fine Arts
Signed '*Dexamenes epoie*', this gem is famous as a masterpiece by the finest Classical gem-cutter and as the first indisputable individualized portrait. The sitter is unknown. The enlargement is from a cast; the original intaglio receives added animation from the play of light.
J. D. Beazley, *Lewes House collection of ancient gems*, 1920, no. 50.

151 *Arkesilas IV of Cyrene?* *c.* 450 B.C. bronze 0·102 m.
Sanctuary of Apollo, Cyrene
Cyrene, Museum
The small head broken from a statue is of incredible liveliness. Assessment of the powerful individual was becoming a problem for Classical art. The diadem may allude to Arkesilas' chariot victory at Delphi (463 B.C.). The identification has been challenged, as Arkesilas was exiled *c.* 455.
Picard 2:1, fig. 83. F. Chamoux, *Cyrène*, 1953, pl. 24:3–4.

152 *Themistocles herm* original *c.* 450 B.C. Roman copy marble 0·50 m.
Ostia
Ostia, Museo Ostiense
Without the inscription 'Themistocles', nobody would have recognized the glorious victor of Salamis (480 B.C.) in this bull-headed, low-browed countenance. Some scholars deny that such an individualized **portrait** was possible before the fourth century; but the style is Early Classic, close to the Olympia sculptures and the *Aristogeiton* (97, 110).
Richter, *Portraits* I figs. 405–8.

153   154*   155   156   157   158   159

153 *Portrait of Phidias*? original 438 B.C. Hellenistic copy marble
Detail of fragment copying exterior of shield of *Athena Parthenos*
London, British Museum
'In making a relief of the battle of Amazons on the shield, Phidias included a figure of himself as a bald old man who lifts up a stone with both hands' (Plutarch, *Pericles* 31). To conservative Athenians, this claim to mythical glory by a living individual was sacrilege.
Richter, *Portraits* 1, fig. 849.

LATE CLASSICAL GREEK SCULPTURE

154 PRAXITELES? *Hermes and infant Dionysos c.* 360 B.C. marble 2·15 m.
Heraion, Olympia, cella, next to its base, 1877
Olympia, Museum
As he brings his baby brother to the nymphs, Hermes stops en route. Teasing, he dangles grapes (now lost) before the future god of wine. In the new Late Classical concept of the divine, the god is unaware of the spectator, and hence remote. The effect was enriched by metal wreath and staff and painting of hair (gold?), eyes, and cloak (purple). About A.D. 170 Pausanias (v:17, 2) saw this group and called it 'art [*techne*] of Praxiteles'. Because of miscutting of the back, use of a strut between tree and Hermes, and high polish, R. Carpenter, C. Blümel and other scholars consider the group a Roman or Hellenistic copy. In my opinion, the *Hermes* is an experimental work by Praxiteles.
H. Süsserott, *Griechische Plastik*, 1938, 148, 360 B.C. Carpenter, *AJA*, 1931, 249 1954, 1, Roman copy. Picard 4:1, 251–302, 343 B.C. C. Blümel *Hermes eines Praxiteles*, 1948. Lullies pl. 228 ff.

155 PRAXITELES? *Hermes and infant Dionysos*, quarter view from the back of 154
The torso, paraphrased after Polykleitos, is awkwardly placed but the view from this angle unfolds a new richness of motion and discloses Praxiteles' quest for a slenderer canon.

156 *Agias c.* 336 B.C. marble 1·97 m.
Family group of Daochos of Thessaly, Delphi
Delphi, Museum

The group included family members of seven generations. Agias won many athletic victories *c.* 450 B.C.; the statue is a hundred years later, hence no contemporary portrait. The more remarkable is the individual, brooding head which contrasts with conventional athletic body. Attribution to Lysippos is conjectural.
Picard 4:2, 620. E. Sjöqvist, *Opuscula Atheniensia*, 1953, 87.

157 *Young boy c.* 350 B.C. bronze 1·30 m.
Bay of Marathon, 1925
Athens, National Museum
An enchanting Greek original, this statue displays the slender canon and rich movement of Late Classical sculpture. The boy gazes at something in his left hand. No cogent explanation of the subject is possible. The soft forms and self-contained mood are close to Praxitelean style.
Lullies pls. 221, VII (colour). Carpenter, *Sculpture* 171.

158 SCOPAS? *Meleager* original *c.* 340–300 B.C. Roman copy *c.* A.D. 100 marble 1·23 m.
Roman villa, Santa Marinella (Punicum)
Cambridge, Mass., Fogg Art Museum, Harvard University
The best copy of a famous work in which the traditional standing athlete becomes a mythical hero defying fate. The original composition included a hunting dog and head of Kalydonian boar. In dispute over the boar's head, Meleager killed his uncle. Meleager's life was then ended by his own mother.
W. H. Schuchardt, *Antike Plastik*, 1963 2:3, pl. 59. Bieber fig. 54.

159 LEOCHARES? *Apollo of Belvedere* original 320 B.C. Roman copy marble 2·24 m.
Found in Rome, late 15th century
Vatican, Musei e Gallerie Pontificie, Cortile del Belvedere
Copied and studied by artists from the Renaissance to Delacroix, hymned by J. Winckelmann (1763), said by J. Flaxman (1816) to be superior to the Parthenon sculptures, 'The Apollo' served for centuries as standard for the European concept of an ideal, divine, Classical beauty. The original of bronze showed Apollo with bow in left, laurel branch in right hand, at once avenger, purifier and healer. Tree-trunk was added by the copyist. The open stance is transitional from the

Classical closed to Hellenistic open form. The attribution to Leochares, Court Sculptor of Alexander, is plausible conjecture.
Bieber fig. 200. E. Panofsky, *Meaning in the visual arts*, 1955, 77. Helbig-Speier no. 226, literature. Ladendorf, 47.

160 *Funerary stele* 330 B.C. marble 1·68 m.
Found near Ilissos river, Athens
Athens, National Museum
The heroic youth who died young broods on his fate, isolated from the sleeping boy and the grief-stricken father. The Hellenistic Age gives up the remote harmony of Classical *stelae* (105). The composition is cleaved in centre; tragic pathos is openly stated and emphasized by contrasts.
N. Himmelmann, *Studien zum Ilissosrelief*, 1956. Panofsky fig. 40.

161 *Mausolos, Satrap of Caria* c. 350 B.C. marble 3 m.
From his funerary temple, the 'Mausoleum', Halicarnassus, 1857
London, British Museum
The democratic Greek *polis* resisted exaltation of the individual. It was foreign rulers whom Greeks first represented as 'supermen'. In this Mausolos, Satrap of Caria (377–353 B.C.) is successor to Tissaphernes. The best sculptors of Greece went to adorn his 'Mausoleum'. The placing of the statues is controversial (on top in a chariot?; in the colonnade of the temple?). Using new psychology and pictorialized marble treatment, the sculptor made Mausolos' head with Iranian hair-do a symbol of massive power.
Lullies pl. 211. Picard 4:1, pl. 2.

162 *Tissaphernes, Satrap of western Asia Minor* 412 B.C. silver tetradrachm diameter 0·016 m.
Hoard found at Karaman, Lycaonia
London, British Museum
The earliest portrait of a living contemporary in ancient coinage, the coin was an imitation of Athenian currency struck to pay Spartans to fight Athens. The ambitious Persian's head replaced that of Athena. A Greek cut the die.
E. G. S. Robinson, *Numismatic Chronicle*, 1948, pl. 5.

163 *Mausolos*, detail of 161

164 PRAXITELES? *Head of Hermes*, detail of 155
In the Late Classical period the states of the soul became a major concern. As Aristotle in *Nicomachean Ethics*, the sculptors consider typical qualities or moods. The *Hermes* is dreaming and relaxed.

165 *Head of Agias*, detail of 156
Thought in High Classical art was unswayed by momentary situation. Its athletes were calm and serene (102, 104). In the new realistic psychology, thought was becoming involved with such 'negative' emotions as pessimistic sadness.

166 SCOPAS? *Head of Meleager*, detail of 158
Defiant courage is another typical aspect of psyche. The strong turn of the head and the deep-set eyes recur in sculptures of the temple at Tegea, of which Scopas was architect. In different views, the head presents different expressions; some anticipate the 'superman' portraits of Hellenistic kings.

167 SILANION *Plato* original (bronze?) 360 B.C. Roman copy marble 0·35 m.
Private collection
A Persian student dedicated to the Muses in the Academy a portrait statue of Plato, then about seventy. No challenge could be greater; the Athenian sculptor's response describes some individual traits and suggests intent concentration, but remains within a typical mould and probes no depths of Plato's genius.
R. Boehringer, *Platon*, 1935. Bieber fig. 116. Hafner fig. 279.

168 SILANION? *Head of a boxer*, profile view of 169

169 SILANION? *Head of a boxer* 330 B.C. bronze 0·28 m.
Sanctuary of Zeus, Olympia, 1880
Athens, National Museum
This superlative head is broken from a small statue. Bits of Olympic victor's olive wreath remain. The old fighter is battered but unbowed. The clear construction, the rich plastic life dominated by rhythmic modulation are still Classic; Classic, too, is the *ethos* portraying an attitude towards life rather than the uniqueness of an individual. Silanion had been praised by ancient critics for a portrait showing 'not

321

170   171★   172★   173★   174   175   176

the man but Anger himself' (Pliny, 34:81). Eduard Schmidt's attribution is plausible, but cannot be proved.
Ed. Schmidt, *JdI*, 1934, 191 ff. Bieber fig. 144.

170 KEPHISODOTOS '*Peace and Wealth*' original 370 B.C. Roman copy marble 1·99 m.
Formerly Villa Albani, Rome; restored by Cavaceppi (1716–99)
Munich, Antikensammlung
A monument of state, the original stood in the Agora of Athens. In ideology, it was an important step from myth to political allegory; in form an adjustment of majestic Phidian goddess to Late Classical concern with casual human intimacy. The woman is 'Peace', the babe 'Wealth'.
Richter, *Sculpture* fig. 149. Picard 3:1, fig. 21.

171 *Athena c.* 350 B.C. bronze 2·44 m.
Storeroom in Piraeus, burned in 86 B.C. Found July 1959
Piraeus, Museum
I. Papademitriou discovered a hoard of Greek bronze statues which were to be shipped to Italy early in the first century B.C. Grace replaces majesty (141, 142) in the image of Athena. Her left hand held a spear and was covered by a shield decorated with chariot races.
S. Meletzis, H. Papadakis, *National Museum Athens*, 1963, pl. 76.

172 *Demeter c.* 350 B.C. bronze 0·81 m.
From the sea, near Knidos
Izmir, Archaeological Museum
Beautiful even when broken, this slightly over life-size image of Demeter grieving for her daughter is a majestic *Mater Dolorosa* of Antiquity.
G. Bass, *Archaeology*, 1965, 7.

173 *Demeter c.* 330 B.C. marble 1·53 m.
Sanctuary of Demeter and Kore, Knidos
London, British Museum
Part of a group with her daughter Kore (124), the noble statue exploits the Parian marble in diversified effects. The best view with head frontal, body turned is carefully calculated. The head resembles Alexander portraits; the artist may be Leochares, Alexander's Court Sculptor.
Lullies pl. 244. B. Ashmole, *JHS*, 1951, pl. 5b.

174 *Victory tying her sandal* 410–405 B.C. marble 1·06 m.
Balustrade of Athena Nike precinct, Acropolis, Athens
Athens, Acropolis Museum
Rejoicings over Alcibiades' victory at Hellespont were not summed up in one Victory (118). On the 'Nike Balustrade' many Victories assume human roles, erecting trophies and bringing sacrifices to Athena. Done twenty-five years after the Parthenon, the 'Nike Balustrade' is an exemplary case of Mannerism: unbalancing, elongating, displacing Parthenonian harmonies. This sculptor excelled in poetry of long swinging folds; they reveal yet hold together the sprawlingly placed body.
Lullies fig. 191. Carpenter, *Sculpture of Nike parapet*, 1929, pl. 27.

175 PRAXITELES *Aphrodite* original *c.* 370 B.C. Roman copy marble 2·04 m.
Original in Sanctuary of Aphrodite, Knidos
Vatican
Head from another copy; neck, hands, feet restored. Praxiteles' persuasive revelation of the natural beauty of a nude woman established Venus as a major theme in European tradition. The copies give little of the melting charms of the original which stood in a small circular shrine (VIII).
C. Blinkenberg, *Knidia*, 1933. Clark fig. 65. Helbig-Speier, 149.

176 *Hera Eileithyia?* 370 B.C. terracotta 0·17 m.
Heraion of Lucania
Paestum, Museum
In the Late Classical Age, old fertility idols (i, *see* p. 12) were often renewed in 'modern' lifelike nudity. The woman attended by Erotes holds Aphrodite's dove. Is she performing a ritual or about to give birth? Hera of the marshes could encompass beauty as well as fertility.
Von Matt fig. 48. Langlotz pl. 131.

177 *Head of Aphrodite c.* 340 B.C. marble 0·288 m.
From Athens
Boston, Museum of Fine Arts
Praxiteles cannot have done better in marble-work. Careful gradations of roughening and refined but not glossy polish result in effects which defy photography. A head composed of large volumes simply outlined; a face sweet yet firm – this is the finest Late Classical head preserved.
Caskey no. 28.

177 178 179 180 181 182 183 184 185

178 *Muse*? *Artemis*? *c.* 350 B.C. bronze H. of statue 1·94 m.
Piraeus, Museum
Found with *Athena* (171). The adolescent girl wears belt and diagonal strap of hunting goddess Artemis; she held an attribute which the discoverer thought was a tragic mask of the same find. The preserved inlays of the focused eyes give her immediate life.
S. Meletzis, H. Papadakis, *National Museum Athens*, 1963, pl. 78.
E. Vanderpool, *AJA*, 1960, pl. 67.

179 *Ariadne*? *c.* 340 B.C. marble 0·41 m.
Sanctuary of Asklepios, South Slope, Acropolis, Athens
Athens, National Museum
This passionate head represents a Scopasian ideal. Because of traces of her hand on the head, some identify her as 'Ariadne *au bras replié*'.
Picard 3:2, fig. 330.

180 *Head of goddess c.* 320–300 B.C. marble
Tarentum
Taranto, Museo Archeologico
Interpreted as Artemis or Aphrodite, this head makes white marble feel soft with delicate *sfumato*, as her shadowed eyes 'swim' in reverie. The firm substructure and clear simplicity of features save the work from sentimentality.
Von Matt fig. 194.

181 *Kreusa*? *c.* 400 B.C. bronze 0·27 m.
Stuttgart, Württembergisches Landesmuseum
The piece is as immediate as a Rembrandt sketch. Bent like a bow, the entire body expresses agony. Kreusa burning to death in Medea's poisoned robe? The unilateral motion is still High Classical, the subservience of body to emotion already Late Classical. Supposedly handle of a vase.
P. Arndt, *Pantheon*, 1931, 79.

182 SCOPAS *Maenad* original *c.* 350 B.C. Roman copy marble 0·45 m.
Dresden, Staatliche Skulpturensammlung
Identified through a poem of Callistratus (third century A.D.) as a maenad swinging a goat she has killed. Introducing a steep spiralling motion, making hair and garment whip round the body, Scopas gave a solution richer in spatial effect, more overtly dramatic than the *Kreusa* (181).
P. Arias, *Skopas*, 1952, fig. 36. Bieber fig. 60.

183 *Dionysiac scene c.* 330 B.C. gilded bronze crater *c.* 0·80 m.
Used as ash urn, grave at Dherveni, northeast of Thessaloniki
Thessaloniki, Archaeological Museum
The *de luxe* vase displays inlaid in silver on the rim the owner's name, 'Astyioulios Anaxagoreos' of Larisa, otherwise unknown. The general shape resembles 'Apulian' craters made in Tarentum. The main frieze, as yet unexplained, shows sileni and maenads one of whom grasps a semi-nude woman round her waist. Four Michelangelesque full-cast figures threaten to glide off the shoulder: Pan and Maenad (back); Dionysos and Ariadne. Scopasian interest in whirling motion (182) is turned into sophisticated Mannerism. The grave also contained armour of a warrior and thirty silver bowls.
G. Daux, *BCH*, 1963, pl. 18. E. Vanderpool, *AJA*, 1962, pl. 107. Boardman fig. 154.

184 *Pan*, detail of 183 from back of crater.

185 *Greeks fighting Amazons c.* 350 B.C. marble 0·89 m.
East face frieze, Mausoleum, Halicarnassus
London, British Museum
Pliny (36:30) says that Mausolos' widow had engaged four famous sculptors; Timotheos, Scopas, Bryaxis, Leochares. Working side by side promoted borrowing hence the attribution of preserved slabs as well as their position on the building is controversial. Scopas appears as leader: Leochares' somewhat softer style (187?) derives from Scopas. Precipitous figures are interlaced in wide arcs. Their rise and fall is more prominent than the beauty of individual figure or the drama of the encounter.
Picard 4:1, fig. 16. Lullies pl. 215 (top).

186 *Charioteer c.* 500 B.C. marble 1·21 m.
Part of frieze from unknown structure, Acropolis, Athens
Athens, Acropolis Museum
This and the two following works are intended to show the variety of Greek sculpture in treating one theme. The Archaic relief, perhaps the

186

187

188

189

190

191

192

193

194

195

same procession as on the Parthenon, spreads in shallow overlapping layers, excels in decorative beauty; the *Charioteer* of the Mausoleum gazes far ahead, his rounded body and swirling robe one stream of motion; the chariot of the golden ear-ring with its ecstatic horses and smiling Victory brilliantly intensifies the Parthenonian contrast (134) of athletic charioteer and demoniac horse.
Payne pl. 127:1.

187 *Charioteer c.* 350 B.C. marble 0·65 m.
   Mausoleum, Halicarnassus
   London, British Museum
   This masterly slab is attributed by some to Scopas, by others to Leochares. Fragments of at least twenty chariots of this funerary race are known; the background was blue and various details painted.
   Picard 4:2, pl. 1. B. Ashmole, *JHS*, 1951, pl. 14. Panofsky fig. 53.

188 *Victory driving chariot* 375–350 B.C. gold 0·05 m.
   Northern Greece?
   Boston, Museum of Fine Arts
   'One of the largest, finest and most complex of Greek earrings' (H. Hoffmann) consists of palmette with suspension hook and pendant (Victory and chariot). The Victory is somewhat more conservative in style than the Mausoleum *Charioteer* (187).
   H. Hoffmann, *Greek gold*, Museum of Fine Arts, Boston, 1965, fig. 12b.

RADIATION TO PERIPHERY: ETRUSCAN

189 *Man and woman c.* 675–650 B.C. bronze H. of man 0·11 m.
   Circle tomb of Costaccia Bambagini, Vetulonia
   Florence, Museo Archeologico
   Preceding the Etruscans, Iron Age 'Villanovans' had developed a Geometric style which lasted into Etruscan times. The enigmatic demons, perhaps beast-headed, embody fertility. For Early Romans, each man had a 'genius', each woman a 'juno' perpetuating life through procreation. For possible models *see* 24, 29.
   Richardson pl. 7; *Geometric* fig. 25.

190 *Sphinx c.* 650 B.C. bronze
   Bernardini Tomb, Palestrina (Praeneste), Latium
   Rome, Museo Preistorico
   Inspired by Near Eastern concepts, this friendly sphinx translates **Near** Eastern calm into energetic loose-jointed geometry. A fitting from a bronze utensil, the piece was found in one of the rich princely graves characterizing the rise of aristocracy in Early Etruria and adjacent regions.
   Richardson pl. 9b; *Geometric* fig. 66.

191 *Nude goddess* 675–650 B.C. ivory 0·095 m.
   Circle grave 'of the Fibula', Marsiliana d'Albegna
   Florence, Museo Archeologico
   The figurine was originally wrapped in gold foil. She holds a cup under the right breast, grasps the left. Her limbs are smooth and well rounded. It was either made by a Syrian craftsman in Etruria or imported, a superior specimen of Oriental art imitated by the Etruscans. An ivory tablet with a Semitic alphabet was found in the same grave whose owner had traded directly with the Near East. The Phoenician Astarte, later worshipped in Etruria, acts here as protectress of the dead. For Near Eastern ivory nudes: *see* Barnett, 105.
   Richardson pl. 11; *Geometric* pl. 10:35–7.

192 *Nude goddess*, view from the back of 191

193 *Head from burial urn c.* 650–625 B.C. terracotta 0·17 m.
   Grave at Castelluccio La Foce, Chiusi
   Siena, Museo Archeologico Senese
   In Clusium, portrait-like heads were placed as lids on jars with ashes – implying that the jar is the dead – a notion much more concrete and 'realistic' than any known in Greece. Such attitude and art may be one of the roots of Roman portraiture.
   Richardson pl. 12; *Geometric* fig. 59.

194 *Goddess on lid of cinerary urn* 650 B.C. terracotta 0·40 m.
   Grave at Chiusi (Clusium), Umbria
   Chiusi, Museo Civico
   Semi-Geometric, semi-monumental, a blind embodiment of grief, the

196

197

198

199

200

201

202

goddess guards the ashes of the dead. A striking group of smaller figurines of mourners and protective griffins stood on the urn's shoulder. *Etruscan culture* fig. 366. Hanfmann pl. 1.

195 *Caryatids c.* 600 B.C. bronze 0·39 m.
A grave at Praeneste, bowl does not belong
Rome, Museo di Villa Giulia
Adapted to stone sculpture (61), exported in pottery from Greece to Italy (Paestum), such caryatid bowls were often imitated in Etruscan pottery. The large-headed goddesses of sheet-bronze grasp breasts with small, incised arms; the disciplined monumentality of Greek 'Daedalic' style is transformed into other-worldly expressiveness.
E. Petersen, *RM*, 1897, pl. 1. *Etruscan culture* fig. 87.

196 *Peleus and Thetis* 540 B.C. bronze tripod stand 0·92 m.
San Valentino di Mariano near Perugia
Munich, Staatliche Antikensammlung
Made by an Eastern Greek in Etruria, possibly at Caere. *Top*, Heracles and lion; *bottom*, Apollo and Tityos; *middle*, Hermes, Peleus, Thetis: the last is turning into a lion. The drama of hero overcoming fearsome disguises to win the bride is turned into a gleeful dance.
Etruscan culture figs. 375, 377. G. Chase, *AJA*, 1908, pls. 12–15.

197 VULCA? *Apollo* 500 B.C. painted terracotta total H. 1·75 m.
From ridge-piece of Temple of Apollo, Portonaccio, Veii
Rome, Museo di Villa Giulia
Staggered the length of the ridge-beam (vii. p. 31), several statues depicted the tug-of-war between Apollo and Hercules who tried to carry off the hind of Apollo's sister, Artemis. Broad of gait, earthy, this Etruscan Apollo is eager vengeance rather than exalted law (96). Probably by the famous sculptor Vulca of Veii who decorated the Temple of Jupiter in Rome after 509 B.C.
Etruscan culture fig. 2. M. Pallottino, *La scuola di Vulca*, 1945, pl. 1.

198 *Athena, Tinia, and giants* 480–470 B.C. painted terracotta 1·15 m.
Revetment of ridge-beam head, Temple A, Pyrgi
Rome, Museo di Villa Giulia
The group mirrors Early Classical Greek experimentation with intertwined motion and exaggerated expression (111, 119). The head of Athena is close to a Greek terracotta head found at Olympia. Only the

broader, coarser faces hint at Etruscan execution. Golden plaques in Punic and Etruscan dedicated the temple to Carthaginian Astarte, equated with Uni, the Etruscan Hera.
G. Colonna, *Archaeology*, 1966, 18, fig. 9. *Athena*: B. Ridgeway, *Archaeology*, 1966, 37, fig. 19.

199 *Winged horses* 350–300 B.C. painted terracotta 1·14 m.
Pediment, temple at Ara della Regina, Tarquinia
Tarquinia, Museo Nazionale
From partial covering (198) the Etruscans proceeded to complete filling of pediment with 'semi-relief' sculpture. The much-restored divine chariot team is rendered as tamed but restive after Pytheos' famous chariot of Mausolos.
Etruscan culture pl. 7. Richardson, 205. Mausoleum: Picard 4:2, fig. 31.

200 *Tinia?* (*Etruscan Zeus*) 450 B.C. bronze 0·405 m.
From Apiro
Kansas City, Missouri, William Rockhill Nelson Collection
The same fierce spirit which animated the *Apollo* of Veii (197) is cast into Early Classical proportions; but one glance at *Hephaistos* (117) makes *Tinia* look tight, angular and linear.
Hanfmann pl. 22.

201 *Chimaera c.* 350 B.C. bronze 0·80 m.
Found in Arezzo in 1553; snake restored by Benvenuto Cellini
Florence, Museo Archeologico
Lean and hungry, snarling at bay, the Homeric monster was probably part of a group with an equestrian Bellerophon. Despite Archaic stylization of muzzle and mane this is a Late Classical work. Etruscan inscription '*tinscvil*' shows that the group was a dedication.
W. Llewellyn Brown, *The Etruscan lion*, 1960, pl. 57.

202 *Head of a youth* 430–400 B.C. terracotta 0·171 m.
Malavolta – Veii
Rome, Museo di Villa Giulia
Etruscan heads are often eloquent and direct. There is heaviness of flesh and spirit in this adolescent. He is fashioned after Classical Polykleitan models but the face of this young Tuscan returns in Donatello's sculpture.
Etruscan culture fig. 122.

203 *Head of a bearded man* 330–300 B.C. terracotta 0·16 m.
Temple at Belvedere, Orvieto
Orvieto, Museo Opera del Duomo
Previously thought to come from pedimental sculpture, now from plaque masking roof-beam end. The figures are inspired by Lysippan style, but no Greek head displays such torn forms, such fierce intensity, as this Etruscan prophet.
H. Jucker, *Exhibition Cologne*, 1956, no. 348. Richardson, 131.

204 *Fleeing girl* 350 B.C. bronze 0·185 m.
San Casciano Fiorentino
Florence, Museo Archeologico
A man's hand grasps her waist. Is she tied to a rock like Andromeda, or is she an acrobat? Her arms were grasping something overhead. The heavy body with small breasts moves as in a dance but the serious expression speaks for an heroic myth.
Hanfmann pl. 30.

205 *Demons and ambush scene* 4th century B.C. local stone
Vulci, Sarcophagus in a grave
The demon-ridden atmosphere of Late Etruscan art is made more ghostly by the gloom of the grave. The scene is slaughter rather than battle. In 358 B.C. the Etruscans of Tarquinia slaughtered three hundred and seven Roman prisoners; in 353 B.C. the Romans decapitated three-hundred and fifty-eight Etruscans (Livy 7:15, 19).
Etruscan culture fig. 107.

206 *Portrait of the dead, a battle scene c.* 150 B.C. terraco'
Tomb at Vignagrande, Chiusi
Worcester, Massachusetts, Art Museum
Placed in front of a curtained colonnade, the battle scene follows with competence the Hellenistic style of Pergamon (237): victors trample on dead, wounded tumble out of the background. The semi-recumbent figure on the lid was imitated from Hellenistic royal scarcophagi, now known from the Mausoleum of Belevi near Ephesus. The powerful head, however, is a striking individual achievement.
Hanfmann, *Worcester Art Museum Annual*, 1947, 15–31. Richardson pl. 45.

207 *Charun*, left end of urn in Worcester (206)
The monstrous takes ugly, devilish shape as in the Etruscan demon of death with lion skin who stands guard at altar in front of the grave. Architecture and armour hung on the wall are remarkably realistic.

208 *Urn of Arnth Velimnes Aules c.* 100 B.C. limestone and stucco total H. *c.* 1·59 m.
Perugia, Mausoleum of Volumnii family
Etruscan sculpture lasted in Perugia until the city was sacked by Octavian (40 B.C.). The subterranean mausoleum contained ash urns of several generations. In a novel solution, statues of two furies are attached to façade of the grave with painted door. The style continues the Hellenistic Baroque current.
A. von Gerkan, F. Messerschmidt, *RM*, 1942, 122–235.

209 *Conjugal couple c.* 300–250 B.C. volcanic stone L. 2·115 m.
Sarcophagus lid of Ramtha, wife of Tetnie
Boston, Museum of Fine Arts
The Etruscans first introduced the motif of the *gisant* into Western sculpture; the house-shaped lid is also a bed. Covered by husband's toga, the couple seems to dance in tender embrace. The portrait of husband exhibits the plainness of Early Hellenistic 'strained' style; the postures derive from elegant Praxitelean dancers.
Herbig pl. 40. Richardson pl. 44.

210 *Velthur Partunus* 250–200 B.C. alabaster
Sarcophagus lid, Tarquinia
Tarquinia, Museo Nazionale
Velthur, who, according to the inscription was eighty-two years old, rests in thought but not in sleep. The simple forms and quiet mood recur in Etruscan bronzes (213).
E. Giglioli, *L'arte etrusca*, 1934, pl. 357:1. Herbig no. 120 pl. 94.

211 *Unknown man* 120–100 B.C. volcanic tufa 0·35 m.
Sarcophagus figure on lid
Copenhagen, Ny Carlsberg Glyptotek
The portrait exemplifies the intrusion of Roman descriptiveness into the Hellenistic Baroque tradition (206, 208) of Etruscan portraiture.
Herbig pl. 98b. *Etruscan culture* fig. 129, colour.

212   213   214   215   216   217   218   219

212 *Head of a boy* 150–100 B.C. bronze 0·23 m.
　　Florence, Museo Archeologico
　　The charming small head belonged to a statue. The prickly detail and
　　the lancet-locked hair compare with the head on 211 and with some
　　Roman Republican portraits. Others date the piece to 300 B.C.
　　CAH Plate Vol. 4, 1934, p. 43a. *Etruscan culture* fig. 123.

213 *Head of a priest?* *c.* 250 B.C. bronze 0·203 m.
　　Bought 1785 in Rome
　　London, British Museum
　　The cap has been taken to indicate an athlete; it resembles, however,
　　the headgear of Roman firepriests (293). The bronze itself seems to
　　flow heavily in this wonderfully expressive head.
　　CAH Plate Vol. 4, 1934, p. 49.

214 *Head of Aule Metelis* 100–80 B.C. bronze life-size
　　Statue found 1573 at Sanguineto in territory of Perugia
　　Florence, Museo Archeologico
　　Disillusioned realism is the keynote of the head of the famous 'Arringa-
　　tore' statue. Etruscan inscription on garment makes the work a dedica-
　　tion honouring the person shown. Roman truthfulness prevails over
　　dynamic play of features. For the entire statue *see* 281.
　　Hanfmann, *Roman* fig. 63. Richter, *Ancient Italy*, 1955, fig. 123.

215 *Head of a man* 80–50 B.C. terracotta
　　Caere
　　Rome, Museo di Villa Giulia
　　Politically Caere became Roman in the third century B.C. Related to
　　'Arringatore', the head marks the stylistic transition to a more penetra-
　　ting concept of the individual in the last years of the Roman Republic.
　　Etruscan culture fig. 131.

RADIATION TO PERIPHERY: OTHER REGIONS

IBERIAN

216 *The Lady of Elche* 4th–3rd century B.C. local stone 0·56 m.
　　Elche near Alicante, eastern coast of Spain
　　Madrid, Prado

This masterpiece of Iberian sculpture displays in a heavy frame of
luxurious jewellery a face which asymmetric painted eyes and pouting
mouth bring uncannily alive. The skill of carving and the controlled
organization of form presuppose thorough Greek schooling.
A. Blanco, *Prado Catalogo de la Escultura*, 1957, pls. 77–8.

GREEK, FOUND IN NEAR EAST

217 *'Penelope' c.* 400 B.C. Greek marble 0·85 m.
　　Main piece found outside, hand and thigh inside, Treasury, Persepolis
　　Teheran, Museum
　　In 480 B.C. the Persians carried the Archaic *Tyrannicides* from Athens
　　to Persia. This marble statue, hacked from its base, was probably
　　booty from Eastern Greece. The general type is known through
　　Roman copies. The 'soft' Greek variant is later than the Parthenon
　　pediments, but earlier than the destruction of Persepolis by Alexander
　　in 330 B.C.
　　C. Olmstead, *AJA*, 1950, pl. 8. E. Langlotz, *JdI*, 1961, 72. E. Schmidt,
　　OIC, 1939, 6.

SCYTHIAN

218 *Scythian extracting arrow c.* 380 B.C. electrum 0·14 m.
　　Vase from woman's burial in Royal Grave, Kul Oba, near Kertch
　　Leningrad, Hermitage
　　The artist observes the Scythian with care in the scientific spirit of the
　　newly developing Greek anthropology. Costume and armour are
　　correct; the sword sheath is like that of 219. The arrow hit the 'patient's'
　　mouth; his doleful face is foreshortened, a device of Late Classical
　　drawing.
　　T. Rice, *The Scythians*, 1957, pl. 4.

SCYTHIAN

219 *Animal contest – battle scene c.* 400 B.C. gold L. 0·30 m.
　　Sheath of sword, Scythia
　　New York, Metropolitan Museum
　　After the originally nomadic Iranian-speaking Scythians established a
　　kingdom in South Russia, artists from Greek colonies on the Black Sea
　　coast portrayed Scythian life for Scythian patrons without showing
　　much response to the excited Scythian 'animal' style. The battle

220

221

222★

223

224

225

226

227★

between barbarians and Greeks resembles those of 133, 185. A sheath from the same mould was found in the princely mound of Chertomlyk about 1860.
Richter, *MMS*, 1932, 109; *Greek Collection* pl. 78c.

HELLENISTIC SCULPTURE

220 *Alexander with lion helmet*, detail of battle scene (*see also* 222).
Clad with the lion helmet of Heracles, swinging a lance, Alexander bears down on a Persian whose horse is collapsing. The conqueror's smooth young face was lit by his blazing glance with painted highlights in his brown eyes.
Bieber, *Alexander* figs. 34a, 36.

221 *Head of Alexander the Great c.* 160 B.C. marble 0·42 m.
Pergamon
Istanbul, Archaeological Museum
Alexander became a legend and the ideal king whom Hellenistic rulers strove to equal. A great sculptor made for the king of Pergamon this leonine warrior; breathing heavily, brow furrowed by strain.
Akurgal, opposite title-page. Bieber, *Alexander* fig. 71.

222 *Alexander's hunt and battle c.* 320 B.C. marble H. relief 0·272 m.
Crypt of Kings of Sidon, Sarcophagus of Abdalonymos
Istanbul, Archaeological Museum
In the sarcophagus of Alexander's appointee, Abdalonymos, the jewel-like brilliance of Late Classical Ionic architecture nearly overwhelms the miniaturistic frieze. The figures are superlatively finished and were painted (VI). In the two pediments, on one end and on one long side, Greeks battle Persians. On the other end and side, they hunt together and Alexander rides to aid a Persian horseman attacked by a lion, probably Abdalonymos; which battles are meant is uncertain. The lion hunt and battle scene preserve the only original contemporary portraits of Alexander.
F. Winter, *Alexandersarkophag*, 1912. Bieber, *Alexander* fig. 35. Picard 4:2, pl. 31.

223 *Head of Alexander the Great* 3rd century B.C. terracotta 0·12 m.
From Alexandria
Alexandria, Greco-Roman Museum
'His neck which was slightly bent to the left' (Plutarch, *Alexander* 4:1) and perhaps the 'lion-like' countenance appear in the lively modelling of this small terracotta head. The heroized type with the Sun God's long locks was created in Alexandria which Alexander had founded. "His tomb was there and he became her tutelary god." (E. M. Forster)
Richter, *Greek Portraits* 3, 1960, fig. 7.

224 *Alexander* original 320–310 B.C. Hellenistic copy bronze 0·17 m.
From Lower Egypt
Paris, Louvre
Usually identified as the type of Lysippos' first (before 330 B.C.) statue of Alexander 'looking up . . . to the sky . . . ' (Plutarch) and holding a lance, but the open stance resembles Leochares' *Apollo of Belvedere* (159, *c.* 320 B.C.). Either Lysippos made the statue after Alexander's death (323 B.C.) or the type was created by Leochares.
Bieber, *Alexander* fig. 18. Charbonneaux pl. 31:3.

225 *Aristotle* original *c.* 330 B.C. Roman copy marble 0·29 m.
Vienna, Kunsthistorisches Museum
Identified through a drawing of a bust in possession of Fulvio Orsini (*c.* A.D. 1600). 'Serious attentiveness dominates; everything is intellectual discipline.' (W. Jaeger.) Methodical observation which Aristotle (384–322 B.C.) contributed to science goes far beyond Plato's portrait (167). Details are refined and fluid, the overall form relaxed.
Richter, *Portraits* 2, 172, fig. 976. W. Jaeger, *Aristotle*, 1934, 342.

226 *Head of Odysseus*, detail of 239 0·45 m.

227 EUTYCHIDES *Tyche of Antioch* original *c.* 295 B.C. marble 0·895 m.
Roman copy found in Tenuta Barberini, Via Latina, Rome, 1780
Vatican, Galleria dei Candelabri
Seated on a rock (Mount Silpius), a boy (River Orontes) swimming at her feet, the *Tyche* by Lysippos' pupil was a revolutionary work, *genre* in appearance, allegoric in content, novel in its three-faced pyramidal design. The copy restored by Cavaceppi (1716–99) has the head from another Roman replica.

228

229★

230   231

232   234

233

235

236★

Helbig-Speier no. 548. T. Dohrn, *Die Tyche von Antiocheia* pl. 2.
G. Downey, *History of Antioch*, 1961, 73–5.

228 CHAIRESTRATOS *Themis c.* 280 B.C. marble 2·22 m.
Temple of Themis, Rhamnous
Athens, National Museum
An inscription on base names the donor Megacles and the local sculptor.
He goes with the anti-Classical current. Justice stands unsure with bent
angular knee. A short, plump upper body rises out of the shell of heavy
cloak with harsh folds.
Horn pl. 6. Bieber fig. 516.

229 *Masked dancer* 250–200 B.C. bronze 0·207 m.
Alexandria?
New York, Walter C. Baker Collection
Clad in transparent cloak, hiding her face under a veil, the ballerina
pirouettes in 'a subtle dance which makes the body fluid and like a
whirlwind' (Pollux 4:100); a dancer for pleasure rather than religion.
The dance provides a natural motivation for a brilliant development
of whirling motion.
D. Thompson, *AJA*, 1950, 371. Bieber fig. 378.

230 PHANIS? *Sacrificing girl* original *c.* 270–250 B.C. Roman copy 1·70 m.
Niche at Arco Muto, Anzio, 1878
Rome, Museo Nazionale delle Terme
The statue was brought to light by a powerful sea wave which un-
covered a niche of the Imperial Villa. A rich relation to space develops
as parts of the figure turn in different directions. There are four distinctive views, but a unifying motion rises slowly from the broad base.
The draperies are beautifully textured. There are vestiges of 'strained'
style as folds work against each other and light and dark make an un-
quiet pattern. She takes something with her right hand from the
sacrificial tray. The small young face is touching in her absorption with
her task. Is this a copy of the *Sacrificing girl* by Lysippos' pupil Phanis
(Pliny 34:38)? The copy is excellent; right shoulder and head are of
finer marble.
Bieber fig. 99. Horn, 56 ff.

231 *Sacrificing girl*, detail of 230

232 *Boy jockey* 230–200 B.C. bronze 0·84 m.
Ancient shipwreck at Cape Artemision
Athens, National Museum
As with Rubens, realism becomes a vehicle to express an all-pervading
life force. The little jockey is seen at the height of the race. To experience the full contrast with the Classic attitude towards a race, turn back
to the *Charioteer* of Delphi (99). A horse from the same wreck does
not belong.
Bieber fig. 645. W. Pasch, *Archaeology*, 1953, 140 (with horse). Hanfmann, *Dumbarton Oaks Papers*, 1963, fig. 33.

233 *Boy jockey*, detail of 232

234 PYTHOKRITOS OF RHODES *Nike c.* 190 B.C. marble 2·45 m.
Sanctuary of the Kabiri, Samothrace, 1863; hand 1950
Paris, Louvre
After their spectacular naval victory over Hannibal off Side (190 B.C.),
the Rhodians gave this statue to the patron gods of sailors. She stood
on a hill high over the sea, on a ship's prow, sailing through a basin
with rocks. Her right hand held a wreath. An inscription on base (now
lost) assured that she is the work of the Rhodian sculptor, Pythokritos
son of Timochares. Every inch a masterpiece of dynamic Hellenistic
Baroque, she displays a novel torsion which 'is checked at waist to be
resumed in the reverse direction in the upper body – Italian Cinque-
cento was to rediscover this device' (Carpenter).
H. Thiersch, *GGN*, 1931:2, 337. Carpenter, *Sculpture* pl. 37. K.
Lehmann, *Samothrace*, 1960, setting. L. Casson, *Ancient mariners*, 1959,
169.

235 *Nike*, detail of 234
The turbulence of folds sweeps and ebbs around her as the sea wind
beats against her wings and her mighty body. (*See* p. 34, viii).

236 *Athena fighting giants c.* 180–160 B.C.
Altar of Zeus, Pergamon
Berlin, Staatliche Museen
Zeus is battling Porphyrion, king of giants; Athena, the youthful
Alkyoneus. Earth, mother of giants, rises in despair from the ground;
Victory crowns Athena.

238

237

239

240

241

242*

243

237 *Zeus fighting giants c.* 180–160 B.C. marble 2·30 m.

East frieze, Altar of Zeus, Pergamon

Berlin, Staatliche Museen

Eumenes II (197–159 B.C.) of Pergamon had received from Rome much of Asia Minor. The Gauls, a terror for almost a century, were discomfited in 184 B.C. This victory was commemorated in mythological sublimation on the altar frieze which narrated the triumph of Zeus, protector of kings, and Athena, protectress of Pergamon, over barbarous giants. To fill almost four hundred feet of frieze, the learned librarians of Pergamon ransacked mythological handbooks and provided identifying 'labels' (mostly lost). Though sculptors came from Pergamon, Ephesus and Athens, the design is uniform, perhaps the work by Menecrates of Rhodes whose name appears with other sculptors' signatures on the base. Here, a generation after *Victory of Samothrace*, the Baroque impetus is waning. The new movement of Classicism leads to a borrowing of Parthenon motifs which, however, is still creative: Zeus is adapted from Poseidon of the western pediment, Athena and Victory from the eastern one (120, *see* p. 27, v). The inventiveness, the skill in interweaving monumental figures, the assured projection and recession, complete mastery of anatomy, the knowing if sometimes theatrical portrayal of passion and pain, make the grandiose frieze the last great monument of Greek relief sculpture.

A. von Salis, *Der Altar von Pergamon*, 1912. Bieber fig. 459. E. Schmidt, *The great altar of Pergamon*, 1965.

238 HAGESANDROS, ATHANADOROS, POLYDOROS *Odysseus' helmsman falling* 175–150 B.C. marble

Cave of Sperlonga

Sperlonga, Museum

A spectacular addition to Hellenistic sculpture came with the discovery in 1957 of a cave transformed into a dining-hall as part of an imperial villa. In two niches with water cascades, and in the centre of a pool, were groups illustrating scenes from the *Odyssey* (x, 404, IX, 317, XII, 85) Odysseus' last ship smashed by storm; the blinding of Polyphemus; Scylla devouring Odysseus' sailors. The clue to interpretation of the groups, pieced together out of seven thousand fragments and now splendidly displayed in a new museum, came from an inscription composed by Faustinus, known as poet of the Flavian emperor Domitian (A.D. 81–96). A Roman copy of the original signatures identified the

artists as the same Rhodian sculptors who made the *Laocoön*. The groups must have been brought from Rhodes or Asia Minor when the cave was refashioned, following its partial collapse under Emperor Tiberius (A.D. 29). The sculptures are even bolder and more dramatic attempts to turn poetry into reality than the *Laocoön*. The style is close to the Pergamon frieze.

Accounts of fast-moving research: G. Iacopi, *L'antro di Tiberio a Sperlonga*, 1963; H. P. L'Orange, *Institutum Romanum Norvegiae, Acta 2*, 1965, *Kunst og Kultur*, 1964, 193.

We are greatly indebted to Dr P. Contecello, Director, Sperlonga Museum, and Professor L'Orange for consenting to publication of these photographs by J. Felbermeyer.

239 *Odysseus and Palladion, cf.* 238

The connexion of the two is not certain (*see also* 226).

240 *Head of helmsman,* detail of 238

241 *Dying giant* original 200–150 B.C.? Roman copy marble

Naples, Museo Nazionale

This detail from the statue of a giant dying, prostrate on his back, displays the same formula of breaking eyes and anguished mouth as the *Laocoön*. Attalos I of Pergamon dedicated (201 B.C.) groups of Gauls, Persians, Amazons, giants, on the Acropolis of Athens; but this style seems later.

Bieber fig. 434. Hanfmann, *Dumbarton Oaks Papers*, 1963, fig. 39.

242 HAGESANDROS, ATHANADOROS, POLYDOROS *Laocoön c.* 150 B.C. marble 1·84 m.

'Sette Sale', Esquiline, Rome, 1506

Vatican, Museums

Attended by Michelangelo, the discovery of the *Laocoön* gave European culture an example of Classical sculpture 'to be preferred to all others' (Pliny 36:37). The group itself was re-pieced by F. Magi in 1960. Less exclamatory than in Montorsolis's restoration, it remains a superlative example of Hellenistic one-view group and 'Pathosformula' (A. Warburg). Comparisons with Sperlonga statuary suggest a later work by the three Rhodian sculptors.

G. E. Lessing, *Laokoon*, 1766, Goethe, "Über Laokoon" *Propylaeen*,

245

248

249★

244

246★

247

1798. Helbig-Speier, 162. H. Sichtermann, *Laokoon*, 1962. F. Magi, *Il ripristino del Laocoonte*, 1960. L. Ettlinger in *De Artibus Opuscula*, XL, ed. M. Meiss, 1961. Panofsky, *Renaissance*, 121.

243 *Heracles fighting centaur* original 150–100 B.C. Roman copy bronze
From Ephesus
Vienna, Kunsthistorisches Museum
Adapted as a torch-holder by the Roman copyist, who added the tree, the group transmits an interesting free-standing composition of the same kind as Sperlonga groups. The 'dancing' rhythm points to declining Baroque phase.
Bieber fig. 639.

244 *Sleeping satyr c.* 200 B.C. marble 2·15 m.
Near Castel Sant'Angelo, Rome, 1625; restored by Bernini (1640?), Pacetti (1746)
Munich, Antikensammlung
In Hellenistic poetry rustics are glorified as healthy, happy nature's children; the mythical follower of Dionysos is shown as a sturdy boy relaxed in sleep. One seems to see how he breathes. Bernini's alterations may have made the work more Baroque than it was.
R. Wittkower *G. L. Bernini*, 1966, 179.

245 APOLLONIOS, SON OF NESTOR *Torso c.* 100 B.C. marble 1·59 m.
Known in the fifteenth century in Palazzo Colonna, Rome
Vatican, Atrio del Torso
Seated on an animal (panther?) skin, the heroic torso is alive with marvellous play of swelling muscles. Emulated by Michelangelo in the *Day* of the Medici Chapel, celebrated by Winckelmann (1759), it was long considered an exemplary 'Classic'. The signature, 'Apollonios Nestoros Athenaios epoiei', is cut into the rock. The subject is perhaps Philoctetes who was deserted by Greeks on Lemnos. The artist had probably paraphrased an earlier Hellenistic group.
A. Andrén, *Opuscula Archaeologica*, 1952, 1. Ladendorf, 31. Bieber fig. 764.

246 *Boxer c.* 100–70 B.C. bronze 1·28 m.
Roman house on Esquiline, Rome, 1884
Rome, Museo Nazionale delle Terme

Blood oozes from his face; the nose is broken, but he remains defiant. The simple posture is Classicistic. The realism of leathery skin and linear hair is lame. There are stylistic similarities to the Belvedere Torso (245), but the alleged signature of Apollonios does not exist.
Lullies pls. 275–7. M. Guarducci, *ASAtene*, 1959–60, 361 (no signature).

247 *Praying boy c.* 300 B.C. bronze 1·28 m.
Mantua; Charles I Collection (passed to Charles II) to 1698; Frederick the Great at Sansouci, 1747
Berlin, Staatliche Museen
In profile the effect of this quiet figure is Late Classical; from the front the upward lift of head and arms brings Hellenistic tension. Tentatively identified with the 'praying boy' by Lysippos' pupil, Boedas of Byzantium (Pliny 34:66, 73). The arms are restored, but position is certain.
Bieber fig. 93. Picard 4:2, 508. P. F. Norton, *Art B*, 1957, 256, note 28.

248 *Hellenistic prince c.* 150 B.C. bronze 2·37 m. without lance
Roman house on Esquiline; with boxer, 246
Rome, Museo Nazionale delle Terme
The sculptor constructs a centrifugal spiral of legs and arms (contrast 117). The sitter was out to frighten. He must be an Eastern prince. No cogent identification has been proposed. The attempt to combine him into one mythological group with the boxer (Castor and barbarian king Amykos) is ruled out by difference of style.
P. Williams, *AJA*, 1945, 330. Lullies pl. 264.

249 *'Borghese' warrior* original *c.* 100 B.C. Roman copy marble 1·99 m.
Imperial Villa, Anzio, eighteenth century. Sold by C. Borghese to Napoleon, 1806.
Paris, Louvre
Signed on tree-trunk by copyist, 'Agasias, son of Dositheos, Ephesian.' Shield raised, sword in right hand, he was fighting a horseman. The sculptor of the original was much interested in anatomy. It overlays the expressive posture like a relief map.
H. V. Hülsen, *Römische Funde*, 1960, 210. *TEL* 3, 263–268.

250 *Emaciated man* original 300–250 B.C. Roman copy bronze 0·115 m.
Near Soissons, France.
Washington, D.C., Dumbarton Oaks Collection

250   251   252   253*   254   255   256*

Find-spot and Roman lettering of inscription, *Eudamidos Perdik*, prove this a copy of a Hellenistic dedication. That the human body was shown as sick reflects the scientific spirit of the Early Hellenistic Age; the empiric school of medicine even practised vivisection. The angular composition is in 'strained' style.
Richter, *Dumbarton Oaks* fig. 291. Lamb pl. 77.

251 *Menander and Archilochos c.* A.D. 30 after Late Hellenistic original silver 0·10 m.
Boscoreale, one of a pair of cups
Paris, Louvre
Under garlands of roses actors and sentiments are explained by inscriptions: Menander, exponent of New Comedy 342–291 B.C. holding torch, 'Life', looks at mask of a hetaera; Archilochos, vindictive iambic poet, *c.* 650 B.C., plays the lyre; large mask on a base is 'satyrplay'; little skeletons play flutes. This is as near as Antiquity came to the Dance of Death. The mood is not 'Repent!', but (inscribed): 'Enjoy yourself as long as you live.' The style is Late Hellenistic Classicism.
Héron de Villefosse, *MonPiot*, 1899, pls. 7 ff. Schefold, 167.

252 *Comic actor and mime* 4th–3rd century B.C. terracotta
Taranto, Museum (the two do not belong together)
Greek humour rarely entered monumental sculpture, but is plentifully represented on vases and terracottas. Many of these are summary but competent sculpture. The masked actor is probably a slave taking refuge on altar; the dancing acrobat is a fine example of Hellenistic grotesque.
Von Matt fig. 33. For the types, Bieber, *Theatre* figs. 410 ff.

253 *Sleeping Eros c.* 250–200 B.C. bronze L. 1 m.
Rhodes?
New York, Metropolitan Museum
Eros has fallen asleep; how peaceful the tormentor looks! The sprawling, slightly ungainly posture is still 'anti-Classical'; the 'breathing life' is already of the Baroque phase. In 1488 Giuliano da Sangallo brought one of the innumerable Roman copies to Lorenzo de'Medici; in 1495 Michelangelo made his *Cupid*, which briefly passed for Antique. It was apparently lost in the fire of the Charles I Collection (passed to Charles II) in 1698.
Richter, *AJA*, 1943, 365. P. Norton, *Art B*, 1957, 251. Mansuelli, 139.

254 *'Capitoline' Venus* original 300–250 B.C. Roman copy marble 1·93 m.
Near S. Vitale, Rome, 1667–70
Rome, Museo Capitolino
In reaction against the Late Classic the sculptor of the original turned the remote goddess into a 'real', selfconscious, awkwardly provocative woman. The compact design has been aptly described as 'impregnable'. The copyist's carving is insensitive.
Clark fig. 66. H. Jones, *Catalogue Museo Capitolino*, 1912, pl. 45.

255 *Aphrodite, Pan, Eros* original 100–80 B.C. Roman copy marble 1·32 m.
Precinct of Poseidoniasts of Berytos, Delos
Athens, National Museum
Pan tries to embrace Aphrodite. Eros tries to push him away. She will hit Pan with her sandal. This group was not found in a bedroom or a bar; an inscription says that Dionysios from Beyrout gave it for himself and his children to his local gods. Homeric gods enjoyed such scenes. The frontal Classicistic composition is intended for architectural setting.
Papaspyridi, 95. Bieber fig. 629.

256 (AGAS?) ANDROS *Aphrodite c.* 150–120 B.C. marble 2·04 m.
Sanctuary of Heracles?, Melos, 1820
Paris, Louvre
In 1820 *Venus de Milo* arrived in Paris to put the stamp of Classical approval upon Neoclassicism. She was thought a work of Phidias. Missing arms and attributes have teased generations of critics into psychologically revealing restorations and interpretations. The sculptor from Antioch on the Meander has combined Classic monumentality with complex motion, yielding a multiplicity of views to make this Ship of State sailing through the waves.
Charbonneaux, *La Venus de Milo*, 1958. Clark fig. 68.

257 *Venus de'Medici* original 150–100 B.C. Roman copy marble 1·53 m.
Rome, sixteenth century. First drawn 1638. Florence *c.* 1677
Florence, Galleria degli Uffizi
Hellenistic Rococo is exemplified in this variation on the Knidian theme (175). Slender upper body, rich hips and coquettish glance: the graceful back is her best view. The support, dolphin and frolicking cupids, are perhaps additions of the Athenian copyist, Kleomenes, son of Apollodoros; arms and hands by E. Ferrata, *c.* 1680.
Mansuelli, 69. Clark fig. 67. Bieber fig. 31.

258 257

260 261 264 266

258

263

259

262

265★

258 *Head of Venus de'Medici*, detail of 257
Despite Classicistic smoothing, the head is alive, especially the foamy, pictorialized hair. But she lacks the refinement of her Late Classical models (177).

259 *Female head c.* 160–150 B.C.? marble 0·33 m.
Found in cistern near Altar of Zeus, Pergamon (237) with hermaphrodite statue
Berlin, Staatliche Museen
A great Pergamene artist took the Scopasian 'Pathos formula' (179) and turned it into fullness of flesh and breathing life, of fluid forms and roughened *sfumato*. She is an implausible companion for hermaphrodite. A Pergamene queen in mythical guise?
Schober fig. 66. F. Winter, *Pergamon* 7, 1908, pl. 25. Bieber fig. 475.

260 *Artemis and satyrs at altar* 120 B.C. bronze
Delos, set into a *stele* at entrance to Temple of Good Fortune
A charming example of miniature Hellenistic relief, Classicistic in empty background and spacing but Hellenistic *genre* in spirit and setting. Polykleitan in stance, carrying two torches, slender Artemis turns a haughty face on the spectator; she is echoed by her statue on tall pedestal; two dwarfish satyrs assist.
Bieber fig. 651.

261 *Cleopatra and Dioscourides* 137 B.C. marble 1·67 m.
Delos, House of Cleopatra and Dioscourides, peristyle
These statues of a Late Hellenistic *bourgeois* couple are seen in the original position in the courtyard of their house. Both types were standard for honorary statues; their symmetrical stances show only slight motion. In a device much used by Hellenistic sculptors, her lower garment is shown through cloak. According to the inscription, Cleopatra had these statues made when her husband gave tripods to Apollo.
J. Chamonard, *Delos* 7, 1922, fig. 95. Bieber fig. 511.

262 *Cleopatra VII* (51–30 B.C.) bronze coin of Alexandria diameter 0·026 m.
Boston, Museum of Fine Arts
'She was the flower that Alexandria had taken three hundred years to produce, and that eternity cannot wither' (E. M. Forster), but the golden image which Caesar set up in the Temple of Venus in Rome and all other statues are gone; the summary coin portraits show a bold profile.
Bieber fig. 364.

263 *Euthydemos of Bactria*? original *c.* 200 B.C. Roman copy marble 0·32 m. From Greece?
Rome, Villa Albani
In this powerful example of dynamic realism 'the modern retouching of the huge nose and skin stimulates the impression of a Renaissance bust' (Bieber). Hellenistic and Renaissance *condottieri* had the same confident attitude 'show me as I am'. Euthydemos had seized a kingdom (222–187 B.C.) in Central Asia.
Laurenzi pl. 29. Bieber fig. 312.

264 *Juba II*? 20 B.C. bronze 0·46 m.
Roman house of third century A.D., Volubilis, Morocco
Rabat, Musée des Antiquités Pré-Islamiques
Found with *Cato Uticensis* (289). The identification as the royal scholar, collector and author, king of Mauretania 25 B.C.–A.D. 23 is disputed.
R. Thouvenot, *MonPiot*, 1949, pl. 9. Braemer, pl. 54.

265 *Homer* original *c.* 150 B.C. Late Hellenistic copy marble 0·41 m.
Boston, Museum of Fine Arts
With heaving forms the imaginary likeness seeks to portray the blind poet, whose genius burns within frail flesh. A glance at *Euthydemos* (263) makes the style of Homer's likeness look soft and idealized. Numerous Roman copies exist; one is shown in Rembrandt's *Aristotle*.
Caskey no. 55. R. and E. Boehringer, *Homer, Bildnisse und Nachweise*, 1939.

266 *Gaul killing himself* original 220 B.C. Roman copy marble 2·11 m.
Rome, Museo Nazionale delle Terme
The savage as hero – the Celtic chieftain has killed his wife and now takes his life rather than surrender. His right and her left arm are wrongly restored. The original composition in bronze, probably by Pergamene sculptor Antigonos, must have been grandiose in its space-encompassing sweep, bold in portraying the high point of physical drama.
H. Schober, *RM*, 1936, 104. Bieber fig. 283.

267
268
269
270
271
272
273

267 APOLLONIOS AND TAURISKOS
Punishment of Dirke original *c.* 150 B.C. Roman copy marble L. 3·08 m.
Baths of Caracalla, Rome, 1456
Naples, Museo Nazionale
The sculptors of the original from Asia Minor were adopted by the
Rhodian Menecrates (Pliny 36:33), designer of the Pergamon frieze.
Made *c.* A.D. 215 to stand in the hall of a Roman bath, the copy is
revealing of Severan taste. The original composition may have had
fewer figures than the copy, but was more complex than the suicidal
Gaul.
Bieber fig. 529. Hanfmann, *JHS*, 1945, 51.

268 *Three Graces* original *c.* 150–100 B.C. Roman copy marble 1·28 m.
Rome, *c.* 1460
Siena, Cathedral Museum
The design may have originated in painting. During the Hellenistic
Rococo it was adopted for sculpture. Mentioned by Boccaccio (1342),
immortalized from Raphael to Picasso, the group has experienced an
amazing variety of allegorical interpretations.
Clark figs. 71, 76, 81, 104. Bieber, 149. W. Deonna, *RA*, 1930, 274.

269 ARCHELAOS OF PRIENE *Apotheosis of Homer c.* 125 B.C. marble 1·14 m.
Found near Bovillae, *c.* 1650
London, British Museum
Using the device of 'groundlines' for even distribution of figures,
'citing' famous statuary, strong on allegory, the little work is an equivalent of learned Hellenistic poems. From top down: Mount Helicon
with Zeus, Memory, Muses; statue of poet (possibly the donor);
curtained sanctuary of Homer; Time and Universe crowning Homer;
kneeling *Iliad* and *Odyssey*; Myth (left) and History sacrificing; Poetry
(with torches), Tragedy, Comedy; Human Nature (child); four
Virtues. All inscribed.
A. Smith, *British Museum Catalogue: Sculpture III*, 1892, no. 2191. Bieber
fig. 497

270 *Building Auge's ark c.* 160 B.C. marble 1·58 m.
Frieze inside colonnade around Altar of Zeus, Pergamon
Berlin, Staatliche Museen
The biography of Telephos, legendary ancestor of Pergamene kings,
was shown in 'panoramic' designs, with figures staggered in height

against continuous landscape settings. Auge (top) and her baby son
will be cast into the sea in the 'ark'. The use of *genre*, the quiet mood
and the soft forms introduce a new concept of illustrated narration.
Bieber fig. 478. E. Schmidt, *The great altar of Pergamon*, 1965, fig. 60.

271 *Lioness and cubs in a cave* 20 B.C.? marble 0·74 m.
Part of fountain frame. Grimani Collection, hence probably from
Greece
Vienna, Kunsthistorisches Museum
The latest phase of Hellenistic sculpture devised an equivalent of small
painted pictures. The dainty, lively portrayal of plants, rocks and rustic
altar is by the same Athenian? workshop as some reliefs of the *Ara Pacis*
(291).
D. Strong pl. 44.

PERIPHERY OF
HELLENISTIC SCULPTURE

SAMNITE

272 *Head of a man c.* 150–100 B.C. bronze
Bovianum Vetus, Italy
Paris, Bibliothèque Nationale
Found in Samnite hinterland, this head from an honorary statue shows
the emotional Hellenistic portrait adapted in some details to factual
Roman taste: stubbly chin, bristling eyebrows; dry, linear – already
Classicistic? – hair. Perhaps south Italian Greek?
CAH Plate Vol. 4, 1934, p. 49b.

CELTIC

273 *God with stag's feet c.* 100 B.C. bronze 0·45 m.
From the sanctuary at Bouray, Seine-et-Oise
Saint-Germain-en-Laye, Musée des Antiquités Nationales
As Romans advanced into Gaul the Celts came into intensive contact
with Italic Hellenistic art. Their creative struggle with Classical anthropomorphism will culminate in Romanesque sculpture. At this early
stage a model similar to the *Head of a man* (272) was assimilated only
in terms of vigorous geometry and violent expression.
Pobé pl. 11.

274

275

277

278

279

280

276

---

274 ANTIOCHOS, SON OF DRYAS
Mousa, wife of Phraates IV 37–32 B.C.? marble
Susa, Persia
Teheran, Archaeological Museum
Cast of features is Semitic; turreted crown ancient Persian; the work is
Eastern Greek of Augustan Era. Signature of artist on crown. The hair-
do resembles that of *Livia* (285). Phraates returned Roman standards
to Augustus (287), sent his sons to Rome. Perhaps goddess or priestess
rather than queen.
Ghirshman fig. 107.

275 CHEIRISOPHOS *Priam and Achilles c.* 20 B.C. gilded silver 0·11 m.
Goblet from chieftain's burial, Hoby, Denmark
Copenhagen, National Museum
Owned originally by a Roman, Silius, this work of Hellenistic Augustan
Classicism exemplifies the extraordinary geographical range works of
Classical sculpture could traverse. The moving scene of Priam kissing
the hand which murdered his son is from the *Iliad*. One wonders what
the Germanic craftsmen thought of it.
Wheeler pl. 1A.

IRANO-HELLENISTIC
276 Mithridates Kallinikos and Heracles *c.* 50 B.C. limestone 3·24 m.
Burial mound of Arsameia Commagene, in place
On towering Nemru Dag kings of Commagene built great burial
structures adorned with sculptures. Inscriptions in Greek claim for
them descent from Persian and Macedonian kings, invoke Greek and
Parthian gods. Greek alliance reliefs provided the design for Near
Eastern covenant of god and ruler. The king's Oriental splendour
contrasts with Heracles' athletic nudity. The style owes more to Late
Hellenistic Classicism than to Parthian linearism.
F. Dörner, T. Goell, *Arsameia*, 1963, pl. 48. Ghirshman fig. 79.

PARTHIAN
277 Satrap before 139 B.C.? bronze 1·94 m.
Temple of Shami, Elam, Persia
Teheran, Archaeological Museum
If correctly dated by Ghirshman, the over life-size statue is an early

embodiment of a new vision of Oriental ruler and a ringing manifesto
of consciously ornamentalized Parthian art. Yet the concept of such a
statue is Hellenistic: 'Stranger, look at the statue of bronze of Zamaspes,
Satrap of Susa. . . .' says a Greek epigram from Susa. The head is cast
separately.
Ghirshman fig. 99. E. Porada, *Art of Ancient Iran*, 1962, fig. 101.

INDIAN
278 Torso of nude *c.* 200 B.C. polished limestone 0·77 m.
Lohanipur, near Patna, India
Patna, Museum
Under Asoka's Maurya dynasty (322–185 B.C.) Greek was an official
tongue and Greek artists decorated his palaces. The amazing transforma-
tion of structured muscularity into flesh at once hard in outline and
softly sensuous in effect must be the work of an Indian who had seen
Greek statues.
R. Ray, *Maurya and Sunga Art*, 1945, fig. 28, dates 50 B.C.–A.D. 50.

SOUTH ARABIAN
279 Eros riding on lioness *c.* 75–50 B.C. bronze 0·635 m.
House of Yafash, Timna, South Arabia. One of a pair
Washington, D.C., Smithsonian Institution and American Foundation
for the Study of Man
Inscribed on base: 'Tuwaybum [father] and Agrabum [son] of the
family [clan] Muhasni'um have inaugurated [the house] Yafash.' The
statues, cast three-quarters in the round from imported moulds, then
attached to a background, are invaluable evidence for Late Hellenistic
style in Egypt. 'Love tames the savage beast'; the playful concept is
carried out in lame Baroque style. For the South Arabians, the groups
probably had entirely different meaning.
R. Bowen, *Archaeological Discoveries in South Arabia*, 1958, pl. 103.

ROMAN IMPERIAL
SCULPTURE

280 Head of a Roman *c.* 50 B.C. terracotta 0·357 m.
Vicinity of Cumae, Italy
Boston, Museum of Fine Arts

335

281

282*

283

284

287

288

285

286

289

This strange and striking head may have been made with the aid of (but not as actual) cast taken from life. The artist made it into a likeness of an age-worn, insecure intellectual. Caskey no. 108.

281 *Aule Metelis c.* 100 B.C. bronze *c.* 1·795 m.
Sanguineto, near Trasimenian Lake, 1573
Florence, Museo Archeologico
The statue is identified as Late Etruscan by its inscription. Heavy-footed in stance, precise but static in execution, it is provincial Roman in style. The worried face breaks Hellenistic dynamism into multitudinous detail (*see* 214).
Hanfmann, *Roman* figs. 48, 63. Toynbee, 24.

282 *Republican general c.* 80–60 B.C. marble 1·94 m.
In substructure of Temple of Hercules, Tivoli
Rome, Museo Nazionale delle Terme
Characterized as military leader by the cuirass, the powerful man is shown with the semi-nude body of a Greek god. A Greek sculptor tried to combine his brand of pictorial Classicism with a heightening of the detailed likeness required by Roman patrons.
Hanfmann, *Roman* fig. 47.

283 MENELAOS, pupil of Stephanos, *Orestes and Electra c.* A.D. 10? marble
Rome, Museo Nazionale delle Terme
Thus might a short tenor sing to a hefty soprano. His 'Classic' torso is hung with a Roman cloak. She paraphrases a Late Classical type. Their faces diffuse *dolce melancolia* to some, to others frigidity. Menelaos was proud to be a pupil of Stephanos, who studied with Pasiteles; with each generation the school turned more Academic and more 'Classical'.
R. Paribeni, *Le Terme di Diocleziano*, 1932, 117. Bieber fig. 787.

284 *Roman couple* 50–40 B.C. marble 1·80 m.
Funerary *stele* from Via Statilia, Rome
Rome, Museo Nuovo Capitolino
They may not look happy but they look real. The rhythmic stances of Cleopatra and Dioscourides (261) are immobilized. His wrinkled brow derives from 'Arringatore formula'; she hoped perhaps to look like Queen Cleopatra. Despite the separating cut, they join in staring down the spectator. Bieber fig. 746.

285 *Livia c.* 10 B.C. painted marble 1·94 m.
Villa of Mysteries, Pompeii
Pompeii, Antiquario
The head was fitted into a prefabricated body which copies a Late Classical type. The resemblance to *Augustus of Primaporta* is striking but many scholars deny that the head represents Augustus' wife (53 B.C.–A.D. 29). Traces of painted black eyes and blonde hair enliven the noble, restrained beauty.
Hanfmann, *Roman* fig. 70. W. Gross, *Iulia Augusta*, 1962, 129.

286 *Livia*, profile view of 285

287 *Augustus of Primaporta*, 19 B.C. painted marble 2·04 m.
Villa of Empress Livia near Primaporta, 1863
Vatican, Braccio Nuovo
Out of the confused welter of Late Hellenistic and Late Republican art Augustus created an art for the Roman Empire. Athenians played a prominent part; Augustus had studied in Greece and later treated rebellious Athens mildly. Two Greek currents were fused in Augustan art, one more Classicistic, the other more pictorial; both were represented in Athenian workshops. But only real conviction could enable these artists to create a recognizably Roman Augustan style. The *Primaporta* type was a successful synthesis of Roman ideology and Greek art; it became *the* official image. On the cuirass is seen the Augustan programme: top, celestial divinities, Sky god protects, Sun on chariot ushers new age. Centre: Parthian (Phraates IV?) surrenders Roman standards to Mars-Tiberius. Sides: pacified provinces, Apollo, Diana. Bottom: bountiful earth.

288 *Head of Augustus*, detail of 287
A high level of idealization is attained without losing individual personality.
Hanfmann, *Roman* figs. 50, 173. Helbig-Speier, 314. Poulsen, 20.

289 *Cato Uticensis* original 50 B.C. copy *c.* A.D. 100? 0·47 m.
Roman house of third century A.D., Volubilis, Morocco
Rabat, Musée des Antiquités Pré-Islamiques
Inscribed in gilded letters 'Cato', the bust immortalized Caesar's

290

292

294

290

292

293

296

297 298

298

291

295*

antagonist (95–46 B.C.). Skull and hair show Classicistic restraint but the contemptuous turn as he 'looks down his nose' and the play of irregular features make a fine character study.
Hanfmann, *Roman* fig. 66. Braemer, pl. 55. Poulsen, 48.

290 *Aeneas sacrificing*, east side of 291 1·55 m.

291 *Altar of Augustan Peace* 13–9 B.C. marble H. *c.* 6·10 m.
Originally under Palazzo Fiano, Rome, excavated 1568–1938—restored and transferred to Via di Ripetta, Rome, 1937
After a century of war, people yearned for peace. The compromise with Parthians (287) removed danger of large involvement in the East. Unrest in the West was settled by Augustus' journey 17–13 B.C. The Senate moved to allay all fears by proclaiming 'The Augustan Peace' on the *princeps*' return. The fears were not idle: while the altar was being built, fighting broke out on the Adriatic and the year of dedication saw the end of Drusus' offensive into Central Germany. The enclosure of the altar emphasized in two friezes the traditional ritual sacrifice and procession and explained the still novel (27 B.C.) Augustan constitution: Augustus, consuls, priests, imperial family on one side; senate and people on the other. That Romans were martial from the beginning was shown by a panel with Mars and the Roman Twins; that they have won all wars, by Roma at peace seated on captured armour. Blessings of peace were detailed by panel showing bountiful Mother Earth (or Italy?) and by rich vegetative display in lower zone of the precinct. This peace was a reward of Augustus' piety – as pious as the legendary founder Aeneas (290). The Attic designer and sculptors used the Altar of Mercy in Athens as architectural model; the Parthenon for suggestions for the frieze procession (103), Hellenistic 'landscape reliefs' for the end panels (271).

292 *Triumphal procession c.* 20 B.C. marble 0·66 m.
Interior, Temple of Apollo in Mars Field, as restored by C. Sosius
Rome, Palazzo Conservatori
This relief celebrates triumph in war. Using even spacing and small figures, sculptors less competent than those of *Ara Pacis* frieze depicted attendants lifting stretcher with two captives and trophy; attendants and three sacrificial bulls. C. Sosius won a Triumph in Syria in 34 B.C.
Ryberg pl. 51. D. Strong fig. 31.

293 *Family of Augustus* south side of 291 1·55 m.
Hanfmann, *Roman* figs. 102–5. H. Thompson, *The Athenian Agora*, 1962, pl. 4b.

294 *The Menorah of the Temple in Jerusalem*, detail of 295 A.D. 81 marble
'And thou shalt make a candlestick of pure gold. . . . And six branches shall come out of the sides of it' (Exodus 25:31–32). During the siege of A.D. 70 the temple in Jerusalem went up in flames. Among the spoils from the sanctuary in triumphal procession in Rome in A.D. 71 was the Menorah of the Herodian Temple. Despite the prohibition of images in Exodus 20:4, its base was decorated with Hellenistic reliefs of eagles and sea monsters. Aware of its symbolic importance the sculptor placed it prominently, gave an almost correct rendering in perspective.
Ryberg fig. 79b. D. Strong 31 ff.

295 *Triumphal Procession, Spoils of Jerusalem* A.D. 81 marble 2·00 m.
Rome, Arch of Titus, southern panel of passage

296 *Triumph of Titus* A.D. 81 marble 2·00 m.
Rome, Arch of Titus, northern panel of passage
Only with favourable sunlight does the relief have Wickhoff's 'illusionistic' effect of momentary motion. Deep relief space and unbalanced composition are devices of Flavian Baroque; the massing of figures in the lower part and the high overhead space were adopted from Early Hellenistic painting.
F. Wickhoff, *Roman Art*, 1901, 78. Hanfmann, *Roman* fig. 109.

297 *Column of Trajan* A.D. 113 marble entire shaft 30 m.
Rome, Forum of Trajan between Greek and Roman Library
Erected as part of the huge complex to commemorate Roman victories in Dacia, this is perhaps the most Roman of all Roman imperial reliefs. Architecturally it has a strange effect, with the groundline encircling the shaft like rope and shallow reliefs piling up in complicated formations.

298 *Column of Trajan*, four lowest windings
The designer drew on an enormous repertory of Hellenistic and Roman figurative motifs; he Romanized them in all factual details (costumes, armour); he elected a scale in which individual human figures still retain

337

299*

300

301

302

303

304

306

305

307

dignity in the Classical tradition; he combined them with accurate if diminished landscape and architecture, and thus created a great epic of the Roman army.

P. Romanelli, *La colonna Traiana*, 1942. Toynbee pls. 39 ff.

299 *Exedra of 'Canopus'* with Roman copies of Classical statues (in casts)
Tivoli, Villa of Hadrian (original statues in museum)
The Romans demoted Classical sculpture from its artistic autonomy and religious purpose to a decorative, mood-making function. Hadrian's outdoor museum is a charming example; statues accentuate a colonnade heightening the effect with their reflections in the pool. 'Antique gardens' from Renaissance to Classicism drew inspiration from Roman suggestions.
S. Aurigemma, *Villa Adriana*, 1961. Hanfmann, *Roman* pl. 1 (colour).

300 *Antinous c.* A.D. 130 marble *c.* 2·00 m.
Tivoli, Villa of Hadrian
Naples, Museo Nazionale
In his life the boy from Asia Minor was worshipped by Hadrian, after death by the entire Roman world. The sculptor softened a High Classical torso to fit it to Antinous' sultry features, idealized after a Late Classical model.
Clark pl. 51. Bulle pl. 82. *CAH* Plate Vol. 4, p. 91.

301 *Mithras* A.D. 180–200 marble 0·36 m.
Cult group, Mithraeum of Walbrook, London
London, Guildhall Museum
Throughout the empire they worshipped him in underground vaults. The group of the Iranian god slaying the cosmic bull occupied there a place 'comparable to that accorded the Crucifix above the main altar of a Christian church. The upward glance recalls the type of inspired Alexander' (Toynbee).
Toynbee, *Art in Roman Britain*, 1962, pl. 42.

302 *Caius Volcacius Myropnous c.* A.D. 150 marble 0·60 m.
Tomb 6, Isola Sacra near Ostia
Ostia, Museo Ostiense
The *Antinous'* artificially softened Classicism and moody pathos and melancholy linger but the downy-faced 'Breather of Myrrh' looks

more determined. Orgies of drill set off his cap of chiaroscuro hair from the smooth face.
R. Meiggs, *Roman Ostia*, 1960, pl. 17.

303 *Sabina as Venus c.* A.D. 130 marble 1·80 m.
Ostia, Museo Ostiense
Hadrian did not get along with Sabina (A.D. 118–38). The sculptor, trained in Trajanic 'factual realism', made one of the most seductive post-Parthenonian Aphrodite types look heavy, but not pedestrian enough to avoid a clash with the young, determined face crowned by Trajanic bird's nest.
Richter, *Three critical periods*, 1951, fig. 134.

304 *Diana of Ephesus*, detail of 305

305 *Diana of Ephesus* A.D. 130–40 gilded marble life-size
Sanctuary of Hestia, Prytaneion, Ephesus
Selçuk, Museum
'All with one voice for a space of two hours cried out "Great is Diana of the Ephesians"' (Acts 19:34). Hadrianic Classicism serves the pre-Greek fertility goddess. The exotic creation has dignity; a firm-featured girl's face looks at the worshipper with appraising glance not devoid of promise.
F. Miltner, *Anatolia*, 1958, pl. 10. Akurgal fig. 108.

306 *Cavalry parade, Column of Antoninus Pius* A.D. 161–5 marble 2·47 m.
Rome, Piazza di Montecitorio, 1703
Vatican, Museums, Giardino della Pigna
The vertical bird's-eye view and the canon of stocky figures has been much discussed. They contrast with Hadrianic Classicism on the main side of the base. One explanation considers the rise of 'folk art' to imperial level; another the co-existence of different sculptural 'modes' in imperial sculpture.
D. Strong pl. 92. Toynbee pl. 43. Helbig-Speier, 378.

307 *Column of Marcus Aurelius* A.D. 180–93 marble H. of frieze *c.* 1·30 m.
Rome, Piazza Colonna, in place
In contrast to the Column of Trajan, the reliefs of the Column of Marcus Aurelius portray war as grim and brutal. The scene shows miraculous rescue of Romans by sudden rainstorm. The rain god,

308

309 310 312

314

316*

315

311 313

developed from a Helenistic wind god type, is a vision foreshadowing Byzantine Pantocrators.

C. Caprino, *La colonna di M. Aurelio*, 1955, pl. 12.

308 *Marcus Aurelius c.* A.D. 165 gilded bronze
From twelfth century near Palazzo del Laterano; since 1538
Rome, Piazza di Campidoglio
As it stayed above ground this equestrian statue became a revered *mirabilium* in the Middle Ages and an inspiration for Donatello and Verrocchio in the Renaissance. Probably set up for victories in the East (A.D. 162–4) the group impresses by the collected power of the horse, by the commanding gesture and calm countenance of the emperor.
Hanfmann, *Roman* pl. 3. Magister Gregorius, *JRS*, 1919, 22. J. Pope-Hennessy, *Italian Renaissance Sculpture*, 1958, fig. 84.

309 *Marcus Aurelius*, detail of 308

310 *Julia sacrifices to Severus and Roma* A.D. 203 marble 1·70 m.
Attic panel, tetrapylon arch, Lepcis Magna
Tripoli, Museum
Lepcis Magna in North Africa, home town of Emperor Septimus Severus, has the first major representation of imperial triumph outside Rome. The traditional sacrifice is regularized in two zones of even figures: Julia (left) throwing incense on altar; then 'Senate, Roma, tall Zeus-like Severus'. 'Concern with welfare of the emperor is metamorphosed into worship of the emperor' (Ryberg).
D. Strong fig. 116. I. Ryberg, *MAAR*, 1955, fig. 89.

311 *Julia Domna as Ceres* after A.D. 217 marble
Piazzale Giulia Domna, Ostia
Ostia, Museo Ostiense
Set on a large body, Hellenistic-Pergamene in type, Julia's (A.D. 193–217) small face fixes the spectator with aggressive glance under the shadow of her wig-like hair. She was worshipped at the grainport (after death?) as Ceres, goddess of harvests.
R. Calza, M. Squarciapino, *Museo Ostiense*, 1962, fig. 28.

312 *Achilles-Penthesilea sarcophagus* A.D. 250 marble 1·17 m.
Known to Giulio Romano 1492–1546; then Villa Giulia
Vatican, Museums, Cortile del Belvedere

The figures look Classical, but within this welter the giant Achilles and symmetrical pairs of Greeks and Amazons are out of scale. Hero and victim imitate a Hellenistic group but have Roman portrait heads. A Hellenistic design is rearranged by abstract 'importance' of actors.
Helbig-Speier, 189. Strong pl. 122. Bieber fig. 279 (Hellenistic group).

313 *Small arch of Galerius c.* A.D. 300 marble W. 2·43 m.
Street of Isaurians, Thessaloniki, 1957
Thessaloniki, Museum
Deeply undercut architectural motifs decorate a Roman arch. Two figures of Phrygian Attis support medallions with a city goddess? and Galerius. Amorini with seasonal gifts fill the spandrels. The outlining of the figures has precedent in Attic sarcophagi of the third century A.D.
G. Daux, *BCH*, 1958, 759, figs. 4 ff.

314 *Persian campaign of Galerius* after A.D. 298 marble *c.* 7·42 m.
Thessaloniki, east side of south pier, Arch of Galerius, Via Egnatia
Although poorly preserved, the reliefs of Galerius constitute important evidence for emergence of imperial court art in the new Greek imperial capitals. The Arch of Constantine (334) squeezed contemporary events into one small frieze; here Greek sculptors strive to fit an extensive picture chronicle into many richly framed panels. From top down: emperor addresses troops; reception of Armenian envoys; Diocletian and Galerius sacrifice; Persian envoys bring gifts.
F. Kinch, *L'arc de triomphe de Salonique*, 1898. Volbach pl. 2.

315 *Priest of Serapis c.* A.D. 230–50 marble 0·288 m.
Egypt
Berlin, Staatliche Museen
Perhaps the most sensitive likeness in the era of transition from realistic Antiquity to Late Antique abstraction: the mood of watchful withdrawal is conveyed with uncanny immediacy by the painted eyes. The lifelike modelling is masterly.
Greifenhagen fig. 108. Toynbee fig. 22.

316 *Flavius Damianus c.* A.D. 180 marble 2·45 m.
Hall of Imperial Cult, East Gymnasium, Ephesus
Selçuk, Museum
Damianus was a famous man of letters. An ample body, a dramatic head, a heavy priestly crown place this Eastern Greek statue between

317

318

319

320

321

322

323

324

the restraint of the images of Classical philosophers (167) and the 'soul portraits' of Byzantine saints.
JOAI, 1932, Beibl. 27. F. Miltner, *Ephesos*, 1958. fig. 67.

317 *Man in toga* c. A.D. 380–400 marble 1·85 m.
Palaestra Forum Baths, Ostia
Ostia, Museo Ostiense
Contrasting with Damianus' Eastern Greek dignity of figure and plastic sense for marble, this gaunt likeness of insecure stance is cut up by tight folds. Made in Rome, it probably represents one of the Neo-platonic pagan senators who led the last intellectual resistance to Christianity.
M. Napoli, *BdA*, 1959, 107. Hanfmann, *Roman* fig. 59.

318 *Constantine* c. A.D. 330 marble 2·60 m.
Apse, Basilica of Constantine, Rome, 1487
Rome, Palazzo Conservatori
Expressionism of the time of crisis was intentionally ugly; the stony Constantinian Classicism eliminates all frailty of flesh and creates a timeless image of 'the divine countenance' whose huge eyes gaze at things everlasting.
Hanfmann, *Roman* fig. 96. Volbach pl. 16.

319 *Emperor Gallienus* A.D. 260–8 marble 0·52 m.
From Rome
Copenhagen, Ny Carlsberg Glyptotek
Gallienus befriended Neoplatonic philosophers; some aspects of his court art show striving for a revival of Classicism, but this colossal image embodies the concept of superhuman ruler in terms of the Late Antique abstracting Expressionism.
L'Orange fig. 8. F. Poulsen, *Katalog over antike Skulpturer*, 1940, no. 768.

320 *Claudia Antonia Sabina* A.D. 215 marble 0·25 m.
Figure on lid of sarcophagus in her mausoleum, Sardis
Istanbul, Archaeological Museum
Femina consularis, great benefactress of Sardis, and probably no stranger at imperial court, Claudia imitates Julia Domna's coiffure (310, 311). Portraits of both women were made by Eastern Greek sculptors, but an expression part sad, part pouting, makes Claudia more human.
C. Morey, *Sardis* 5:1, 1924, fig. 10; *Early Christian art*, 1942, 24.

321 *Portrait of a lady* A.D. 240–50 marble 0·50 m. with bust
Alexandria, Greco-Roman Museum
Set in Antiquity on a gorgeously attired bust (fourth century A.D.), this fine head with painted eyes recalls the *Priest of Serapis* (315), but goes beyond in simplification of form and incipient 'heavenward gaze'.
P. Graindor, *Bustes et statues-portraits*, 1939, no. 57. Reutersward pl. 19.

ROMAN SCULPTURE
Roman provincial

ROMAN GAUL
322 *Head of a Helvetian* 2nd century A.D. gilded bronze 0·15 m.
From Aventicum
Avenches, Musée romain
The Romans had inherited Hellenistic approach to ethnography in science and Hellenistic typology of Barbarians in art. Tacitus' *Germania* in literature, the Column of Trajan in art, mark the beginning of a more direct observation which, in masterpieces such as this, leads to powerful characterizations unprecedented in Greek art.
Braemer, pl. 39. Pobé pl. 198.

ROMAN BRITAIN
323 *Head-pot depicting woman* early 3rd century A.D. terracotta 0·292 m.
Fishergate, Eboracum (York)
York, Yorkshire Museum
The *Head of a Helvetian* utilized resources of Classic sculptural tradition; this pot is essentially a statement of 'native' expressionism. It owes to Roman art only the general stimulus towards anthropomorphism and the details of Severan coiffure.
J. M. C. Toynbee, *Art in Roman Britain*, 1962, pl. 194.

ROMAN BRITAIN
324 *Emperor Claudius?* c. A.D. 50 bronze 0·33 m.
From River Alde, Rendham, Suffolk
Benhall Lodge, Saxmundham, Suffolk
The head was violently hacked from body, probably during the sack of Camulodunum by Queen Boadicea in A.D. 61. The work of a Gaulish artist, this image of conqueror of Britain – if it be he – is instruc-

325

327   328

329

330

326

331

tive for the simplifying, abstract tendency seen here long before it appeared in Rome.

J. M. C. Toynbee, *Art in Roman Britain*, 1962, pl. 7.

ROMAN BRITAIN

325 *Face-mask helmet c.* A.D. 100 bronze 0·28 m.
Bremetennacum (Ribchester), Lancashire
London, British Museum
This is what a soldier of Trajan wanted to look like. 'Worn by auxiliary horsemen in the Roman army for tournaments and exercise' (Toynbee), these helmets are important reflections of the military ideal. They often display gorgeous decorative reliefs: seated figures, sea monsters, heads, infantry and cavalry.
J. M. C. Toynbee, *Art in Roman Britain*, 1962, pl. 108.

ROMAN GAUL

326 *Lion attacking gladiator* 1st century A.D. limestone 1·10 m.
Chalon-sur-Saône
Chalon-sur-Saône, Musée Denon
The Gallo-Roman sculptor transforms a scene from Roman amphitheatre into a symbol of monstrous power overcoming helpless humanity. The lion is a Proto-Romanesque embodiment of evil: '*si non fugies salvus non eris*; *ecce leones*' (Medieval inscription).
Braemer, pl. 63.

ROMAN GAUL

327 *Altar to the Aufanian Mothers* A.D. 164 limestone W. 0·85 m.
Near the Cathedral, Bonn
Bonn, Rheinisches Landesmuseum
Dedicated by *quaestor*, Vettius Severus, to Celtic goddesses whose festival occurred on 24 December. Apsidal shrine; donor's family behind screen; small consular date at bottom. Designed like a manuscript page, the monument shows the successful synthesis of native belief and Classical form achieved by leading Gallo-Roman *ateliers*.
H. von Schoppa, *Die Kunst der Römerzeit in Gallien*, 1957, pl. 82.

PALMYRENE

328 *Funerary portraits c.* A.D. 175–200 limestone
Mausoleum of Yarhai, Palmyra, 1934. Reconstructed
Damascus, Museum

'And Abraham begat. . . .' The ladder of generations gives ultimate meaning and artistic effect to Palmyrene sculpture: within the rich architectural order of their burial towers, row upon row of icon-like images stare into eternity.
Ghirshman fig. 83.

Roman periphery

GANDHARAN

329 *Standing Buddha c.* A.D. 100
Formerly in the Guides' Mess, Hoti-Mardan, near Peshawar
Greek sculpture in its Roman refraction provided the images of two founders of world religions – Christ and Buddha. Memories of Greek Apollos may be discovered in the head; the body is modelled upon toga-clad Romans.
B. Rowland, *The art and architecture of India*, 1953, pl. 31.

GANDHARAN

330 *Buddha's great renunciation* 2nd century A.D. schist 0·475 m.
Swat Valley
Calcutta, Indian Museum
Like the preceding statue a monument of Gandharan art (northwest Indian) which developed under Scythian Kushan dynasty. Subject, content and detail is Buddhist, but the overall design adapted Roman imperial reliefs and perhaps an equestrian statue (*see* 306).
Cleveland Museum, *Ancient sculpture from India*, 1965, no. 48.

LATE ROMAN AND EARLY CHRISTIAN SCULPTURE

331 *Good Shepherd c.* A.D. 250 marble 0·81 m.
La Gayole; reused sixth century, Tomb of Syagria, Merovingian chapel
Varennes, France, Church of Brignoles
Already about A.D. 200 Christians drank Eucharist from chalices adorned with the Good Shepherd (John 10:2; Tertullian, *De pudicitia* 10). The shepherd and praying woman shown above make the relief Christian. The seated philosopher may be St Paul. The rounded, plastic workmanship is Asiatic Greek.
Pobé pl. 227.

332 333 334* 335 336 337 338 339

COPTIC

332 *Daniel in the lions' den c.* A.D. 500 ivory pyxis relief 0·09 m.
Washington, D.C., Dumbarton Oaks Collection
'Copts' were Egypt's Christians, mostly believers in one nature of Christ. Alexandria, seat of the Patriarch, may have originated ivories in somewhat dry style. Daniel's ecstatic pose is Early Christian; the angel, who neatly muzzles the lion, is a distant descendant of the *Victory of Samothrace* (234).
Brooklyn Museum, *Pagan and Christian Egypt,* 1941, no. 105.

COPTIC

333 *Dancing nereids* 5th century A.D. limestone 0·60 m.
Ahnas
Trieste, Civico Museo di Storia ed Arte
The emergence of monumental Coptic sculpture in Egypt from Late Roman provincialism is sudden and strikingly uniform. Tenaciously retained mythological themes display weightless Chagallesque figures which are ornamentalized and interwoven in light and dark pattern.
Villa Hügel, Essen, *Koptische Kunst,* 1963, pl. 80.

334 *Arch of Constantine* A.D. 312–15 brick and marble 21 m.
Rome, for victory over Maxentius at Milvian Bridge, north side
Imposing in its architectural effect, the arch is decorated with statues and reliefs taken from earlier monuments of 'good' emperors: Trajan, Hadrian, Marcus, whose heads were replaced by those of Constantine and Licinius. Only the bases, spandrels, ends and the inconspicuous friezes under the medallions are Constantinian. Consciously traditional, religiously neutral, it commemorates that victory which made Constantine support Christianity.
Hanfmann, *Roman* fig. 140. L'Orange, *Der spätantike Bildschmuck,* 1939.

335 *People listening to Constantine,* detail of 334 1·02 m.
On the speaker's platform are senators; below, the people. The platform shows railings with herms, seated statue of Emperor Antoninus Pius. The Roman Forum is described by the platform, the arch and columns with statues. The sculptor individualizes the heads, schematizes the dumpy bodies.
D. Strong pl. 137. Volbach pl. 15.

336 *Sarcophagus of Constantia c.* A.D. 330 porphyry 2·25 m.
S. Costanza, Rome
Vatican, Museums, Sala della Croce Greca
Lambs and peacocks might be Christian. The vintaging *putti* were 'neutral'. There were reasons for cautious imagery. Constantine's religious advisor, Eusebius, had rebuked Constantia when she asked for an image of Christ. The piece copying Constantine's casket was carved in Egypt, where porphyry was brought from Mount Sinai.
Volbach pl. 24. Helbig-Speier, 17. A. Vassiliev, *Dumbarton Oaks Papers,* 1948, fig. 17.

337 *Sarcophagus* A.D. 385–90 marble 1·14 m.
Milan, S. Ambrogio (SS. Protasius and Gervasius, founded A.D. 386)
Lid: ox and ass adoring the Babe. End: Elisha-Elija, Adam-Eve, Noah, Moses. Front: Mission of the Apostles; deceased couple kissing Christ's feet; Agnus Dei and twelve lambs. Background: city gates, 'Holy City, the new Jerusalem coming down from God' (Rev. 21:2); the Church with twelve apostolic gates (St Ambrose). A comprehensive dogmatic programme with multiple meanings is realized in stately figures loosely disposed in Old Testament scenes of the end, rhythmical, centralized in 'Church as Salvation' theme of the front. Created in the circle of St Ambrose, bishop (374–97), when Milan was imperial residence.
Volbach pl. 46. A. Katzenellenbogen, *Art B,* 1947, 249 (exegesis).

338 *Sarcophagus of Adelfia c.* A.D. 340 marble originally painted
In a recess of the 'Rotunda di Adelfia' in 1872
Syracuse, Museo Archeologico
As Christianity became fashionable, sarcophagi for aristocrats became elaborate; Adelfia and Count Valerius are larger than the Lord. The condensed miracles (top) of earlier Christian frieze sarcophagi are amplified by scenes of Old and New Testaments in lower register and on lid.
Volbach pl. 37. G. Bovini, *Sarcofagi paleocristiani,* 1949, fig. 233.

339 *Sarcophagus of Junius Bassus* A.D. 359 marble 2·43 m.
Confessio, Old St Peter's, Rome, 1595
Vatican, Crypt of St Peter
Twenty years after Adelfia, Bassus, who as *praefectus urbi* held Rome's highest position, ordered his sarcophagus from a court sculptor trained in Asia Minor. Luxurious in effect, Classic in its statuesque groups,

340

342 343

344

345

346

347

348

341

the design is also a much clearer exposition of Christian iconography.
F. Gerke, *Sarkophag des Junius Bassus*, 1936. Volbach pl. 41.

340 *Adam and Eve*, detail of 339
What was sacred became shameful. To express shame the artist took a
Venus pudica, made a nude athlete repeat her gesture. Averted gazes
are to indicate despair. Faced with total re-evaluation of nudity, the
artist could not quite suppress his admiration of ancient statues; though
awkward, his bodies are not vessels of sin and decay.

341 *Death of Judas: Crucifixion c.* A.D. 420 ivory 0·075 m.
London, British Museum
Two deaths – the dead tree and the living cross; the Brueghelian
soldier; the heavy gesture of Thomas; Mary's grief-swollen face. In
daring to show the ultimate mystery the artist overloads his short,
homely people with feeling and meaning.
Volbach pl. 98. E. Bevan, *Holy Images*, 1940, pl. 2.

342 *Orpheus charming animals* A.D. 350–400 marble 1·10 m.
Athens, Byzantine Museum
Under an open-work arch of animals surmounted by an eagle, this
immobilized Orpheus resembles portraits of Constantius (345).
Orpheus was paralleled with Christ in several ways: he came back from
Hell; when he sang, lion and lamb lay down together; he tamed wild
beasts (pagans): overcame beasts (sinful passions). Yet this Late Antique
sculpture need not be Christian.
S. Sotiriou, *Guide du Musée byzantin*, 1932, fig. 17.

343 *Youthful Christ teaching c.* A.D. 350 marble 0·72 m.
Rome, Museo Nazionale delle Terme
Early Christian visions of Christ varied from infant to benign old man,
from small and humble to a giant 'who towered above the pediment of
the amphitheatre' (S. Perpetua). Here Christ is long-locked like sun god
('Sun of Salvation'), clad like philosopher. For 'soft' style cf. 339.
W. Visser, *Entwicklung des Christusbildes*, 1934. Volbach pl. 98.

344 *Triumphant emperor* 6th century A.D. bronze head *c.* 0·85 m.
From Constantinople, 1204?
Barletta, in front of S. Sepolcro
The tallest bronze statue of Antiquity was attired in imperial armour.

The face is furrowed, tense, ascetic; all features draw towards the eyes.
His gaze seeks guidance from above. Identification is controversial.
Peirce I, pl. 32. Volbach pl. 70. Beckwith fig. 38.

345 *Constantius II* A.D. 324–61 bronze 1·77 m.
In the Middle Ages, near the Lateran until 1471
Rome, Palazzo Conservatori, Sala dei Bronzi
The colossal head retains Constantine's grandiose immobility but shows
in big nose and jutting chin the last 'Roman profile'. The heavy,
Germanic-style bolster of hair and the (lost) crown created a more
ornate, Medieval impression.
Hanfmann, *Roman* fig. 95. Volbach pl. 18.

346 *Evangelist* 5th century A.D. marble 0·69 m.
Fatih, Istanbul, with three Evangelist medallions
Istanbul, Archaeological Museum
One of the few sculptures of competence attesting the formation of a
Constantinopolitan style. No longer is the Evangelist a Christianized
philosopher; circling folds and gesture lead to the Book and the Cross,
an integral part of the composition.
Volbach pl. 74. Beckwith fig. 35.

347 *Adoration of Magi c.* A.D. 420 marble 0·69 m.
Reused, lid added before A.D. 650 for Exarch Isaac
Ravenna, S. Vitale
The sculptor planned 'Classical' rhythm, spacing and glances but
showed Madonna as a real Mediterranean mother, veiled head to foot,
tightly holding the eager Child. To replace the central figure of Christ
with this scene meant special glorification of the Virgin.
M. Lawrence, *Sarcophagi of Ravenna*, 1945, fig. 12. Volbach pl. 179.

348 *Heracles and Nemean lion* 6th century A.D. silver diameter 0·60 m.
From Trivulzio Collection, Milan
Paris, Cabinet des Médailles
A Classical statuary group, first adopted in Hellenistic reliefs, then
transposed into Roman silverware, finally appears on this silver plate
of the time of Justinian. Space and anatomy are distorted; all is jewelled
decoration, but the Classical components are outlined with remarkable
faithfulness. Forsetting (tree) *see* 271
Volbach pl. 251. Compare coin of 380 B.C., von Matt fig. 175.

343

BIBLIOGRAPHY

Publishers listed are those whose editions are quoted in the Notes.

Akurgal, E., *Die Kunst Anatoliens*, De Gruyter, Berlin, 1961

Barnett, R., *The Nimrud ivories*, Trustees of the British Museum, London, 1957

Beckwith, J., *Coptic sculpture*, Alec Tiranti, London, 1963

Bieber, M., *Sculpture of the Hellenistic Age*, Columbia University Press, New York, 1961

   Alexander the Great in Greek and Roman art, Argonaut, Chicago, 1964

   The history of the Greek and Roman theatre, Princeton University Press, Princeton, New Jersey, 1961

Blümel, C., *Die archaisch griechischen Skulpturen der Staatlichen Museen zu Berlin*, Akademie Verlag, Berlin, 1964

Boardman, J., *Greek art*, Thames and Hudson, London, 1964

Boston, Museum of Fine Arts, *Greek, Etruscan and Roman art*, Harvard University Press, Cambridge, Mass., 1963

Braemer, F., *L'art dans l'occident romain*, Louvre Exhibition, 1963, Ministère d'État affaires culturelles, Paris, 1963

Brommer, F., *Die Skulpturen der Parthenon-Giebel*, Philipp von Zabern, Mainz, 1963

   Die Giebel des Parthenon, Philipp von Zabern, Mainz, 1959

Bulle, H., *Der schoene Mensch im Altertum*, G. Hirth, Munich and Leipzig, 1912

Buschor, E., *Altsamische Standbilder I–V*, Gebr. Mann, Berlin, 1934–61

Carpenter, R., *Greek sculpture*, University of Chicago Press, Chicago, 1960

   Greek art, Pennsylvania University Press, Philadelphia, 1962

Caskey, L. D., *Catalogue of Greek and Roman sculpture*, Museum of Fine Arts, Boston, Harvard University Press, Cambridge, Mass., 1925

Charbonneaux, J., *Greek bronzes*, Viking, New York, 1962

   La sculpture grecque archaïque, Éditions de Cluny, Paris, 1938

Clark, K., *The nude*, Doubleday Anchor, New York, 1956

Corbett, P., *The sculpture of the Parthenon*, Penguin Books, Harmondsworth, 1959

Demargne, P., *Naissance de l'art grec*, Editions Gallimard, Paris, 1964

Fogg Art Museum, *Ancient art in American private collections*, Stinehour Press, Vermont, 1954

Ghirshman, R., *Persian art*, Golden Press, New York, 1962

Greifenhagen, A., *Antike Kunstwerke*, De Gruyter, Berlin, 1960

Hafner, G., *Geschichte der griechischen Kunst*, Atlantis Verlag, Zürich, 1961

Hanfmann, G. M. A., *Etruskische Plastik*, H. E. Günther, Stuttgart, 1956

   Roman art, New York Graphic Society, Greenwich, Conn., 1964

Haynes, D., *An historical guide to the sculptures of the Parthenon*, Trustees of the British Museum, London, 1962

Helbig, W., *Führer durch die öffentlichen Sammlungen klassischer Altertumer in Rom*, 4th ed. by H. Speier, Ernst Wasmuth, Tübingen, 1963

Herbig, R., *Die jüngeretruskischen Steinsarkophage*, Gebr. Mann, Berlin, 1952

Himmelmann-Wildschütz, N., *Bemerkungen zur geometrischen Plastik*, Gebr. Mann, Berlin, 1964

Horn, R., *Stehende weibliche Gewandstatuen in der hellenistischen Plastik*, Ergänzungsheft II, RM, Deutsches Archäologisches Institut, Berlin, 1931

Jeffery, L., *Local scripts of Greece*, Oxford University Press, London, 1961

Karo, G., *An Attic cemetery*, Oberlaender Trust, Philadelphia, 1943

Kunze, E., *Bericht über die Ausgrabungen in Olympia*, Deutsches Archäologisches Institut, Berlin, 1956–58

Ladendorf, H., *Antikenstudium und Antikenkopie*, Akademie Verlag, Berlin, 1953

Lamb, W., *Greek and Roman bronzes*, Methuen, London, 1929

Langlotz, E., *Die Kunst der Westgriechen in Sizilien und Unteritalien*, Hirmer Verlag, Munich, 1963

Laurenzi, L., *Ritratti greci*, Sansoni, Florence, 1941

L'Orange, H. P., *Studien zur Geschichte des spätantiken Porträts*, Williams and Norgat, London, 1933

Lullies, R., *Greek sculpture*, H. Abrams, New York, 1960

Mansuelli, G. A., *Galleria degli Uffizi, La sculpture I*, Istituto Poligrafico dello Stato, Rome, 1958

Marcadé, J., *Recueil des signatures des sculpteurs grecs*, Librairie Boccard, Paris, vol. 1, 1953, vol. 2, 1957

Marinatos, S., *Crete and Mycenae*, H. Abrams, New York, 1960

Matz, F., *Geschichte der griechischen Kunst*, Vittorio Klostermann, Frankfurt, 1950

Müller, V., *Frühe Plastik in Griechenland und Vorderasien*, Dr Benno Filser Verlag, Augsburg, 1929

Panofsky, E., *Tomb sculpture*, H. Abrams, New York, 1964

   Renaissance and renascences in Western art, Almquist and Wiksell, Stockholm, 1960

Papaspyridi, S., *Guide du Musée National d'Athènes*, Maison d'Éditions 'Eleftheroudakis', Athens, 1927

Payne, H., *Archaic marble sculpture of the Acropolis*, W. Morrow & Co., New York, 1950

   Protokorinthische Vasenmalerei, H. Keller, Berlin, 1933

Peirce, H., and Tyler, R., *L'art byzantin*, Librairie de France, Paris, 1932–34

Picard, C., *Manuel d'archéologie grecque, la sculpture*, 1–4, Éditions Auguste Picard, Paris, 1935–54

Platon, N., *A guide to the archaeological museum of Heraklion*, Heraklion, Crete, 1959

Pliny the Elder's chapters on history of art, K. Jex-Blake, E. Sellers ed., Macmillan, London, New York, 1896

Pobé, M., and Roubier, J., *The art of Roman Gaul*, University of Toronto Press, Toronto, 1961

Pollitt, J., *The art of Greece, 1400–31 B.C.*, Prentice Hall, New Jersey, 1965

Poulsen, V., *Les portraits romains I*, Publications de la Glyptothèque Ny Carlsberg, Copenhagen, 1962

Pryce, F. N., *Catalogue of sculptures*, British Museum, London, 1928

Reuterswürd, P., *Studien zur Polychromie der Plastik*, Almquist and Wiksell, Stockholm, 1960

Richardson, E., *The Etruscans*, University of Chicago Press, 1964
    'Recurrent Geometric in the sculpture of Italy, and its bearing on the origin of the Etruscans', *MAAR*, 1962

Richter, G. M. A., *Catalogue of Greek and Roman antiquities in the Dumbarton Oaks Collection*, Harvard University Press, Cambridge, Mass., 1956
    The Archaic gravestones of Attica, Phaidon Press, London, 1961
    Handbook of the Greek collection, Metropolitan Museum of Art, Harvard University Press, Cambridge, Mass., 1953
    Handbook of Greek art, Phaidon Press, London, 1960
    Kouroi, Archaic Greek youths, Phaidon Press, London, 1960
    The portraits of the Greeks I–III, Phaidon Press, London, 1965
    Sculptors and sculpture of the Greeks, Yale University Press, New Haven, Conn., 1950

Rowland, R., *The classical tradition in western art*, Harvard University Press, Cambridge, Mass., 1963

Ryberg, I., 'Rites of the Roman State religion', *MAAR*, 1955

Schefold, K., *Die Bildnisse der antiken Dichter, Redner und Denker*, Benno Schwabe, Basel, 1943

Schober, A., *Die Kunst von Pergamon*, Friedrich Rohrer, Vienna, 1951

Schrader, H., and Langlotz, E., *Die archaischen Marmorbildwerke der Akropolis*, Vittorio Klostermann, Frankfurt, 1939

Smith, A. H., *Catalogue of the sculptures of the Parthenon*, London, 1900

Strong, D., *Roman imperial sculpture*, Alec Tiranti, London, 1961

Swedish Archaeological Institute, Rome, *Etruscan culture*, Columbia University Press, New York, 1962

Toynbee, J. M. C., *The art of the Romans*, Thames and Hudson, London, 1965

Vermeule, E., *Greece in the Bronze Age*, University of Chicago Press, Chicago, 1964

Volbach, W., *Early Christian art*, H. Abrams, New York, 1961

Von Matt, L., *Magna Graecia*, Universe Books, New York, 1962

Wheeler, Sir M., *Rome beyond the imperial frontiers*, G. Bell, London, 1954

Yalouris, N., *Classical Greece*, New York Graphic Society, Greenwich, Conn., 1960

Zervos, C., *Naissance de la civilisation en Grèce*, Éditions Cahiers d'Art, Paris, 1962–3
    L'art des Cyclades, Éditions Cahiers d'Art, Paris, 1957

INDEX AND GUIDE TO LOCATION

The Index includes periods (or styles), titles or subjects of the sculptures, materials and find-places. Numbers in bold type refer to the actual picture; numbers in *italics*, following the page numbers, refer to the Notes on, and other references to, the illustrations.

The Guide to Location is a list of towns, museums and other places where the sculptures are now situated. Numbers refer to the illustrations.

INDEX

347

GUIDE TO LOCATION